SAINT THÉRÈSE OF LISIEUX

BERNARD BRO

Saint Thérèse of Lisieux

Her Family
Her God
Her Message

Translated by
Anne Englund Nash

IGNATIUS PRESS   SAN FRANCISCO

Title of the French original:
Thérèse of Lisieux: Sa famille, son Dieu, son message
© 1996 Librairie Arthème Fayard

Cover photograph:
Thérèse Martin at 15 years
© Office Central de Lisieux

Cover design by Riz Boncan Marsella

© 2003 Ignatius Press, San Francisco
ISBN 0–89870–842–7
Library of Congress Control Number 2003103052
Printed in the United States of America ◯

Contents

Abbreviations

CG   *Correspondance générale de Thérèse de Lisieux* (Cerf/ DDB, 1972/1974); revised and edited in the *Nouvelle Édition du Centenaire* (1992).

CSG   *Conseils et souvenirs*, published by Sister Geneviève (Céline).

DE   *Derniers Entretiens* (Cerf/DDB, 1972); revised and reprinted in NEC (1992).

GC   Saint Thérèse of Lisieux. *General Correspondence.* Translated by John Clarke, O.C.D. 2 vols. Washington, D.C.: ICS Publications, Institute of Carmelite Studies, 1982–1988.

HA   *Histoire d'une Âme* [Story of a soul], 1898 (1907; 1972, etc.).

LC   *St. Thérèse of Lisieux: Her Last Conversations.* Translated by John Clarke, O.C.D. Washington, D.C.: ICS Publications, Institute of Carmelite Studies, 1977.

LT   Letters from Thérèse: see GC

NEC   *Nouvelle Édition du Centenaire des Œuvres complètes de Thérèse de Lisieux* [New centenary edition of the Complete works of Thérèse of Lisieux] (Cerf/ DDB, 1991), in 8 volumes.

NPPA   *Notes préparatoires au Procès Apostolique* [Preparatory notes for the apostolic process].

NPPO   *Notes préparatoires au Procès de l'Ordinaire* [Preparatory notes for the bishop's process].

PA   *Procès Apostolique* [apostolic process], 1915–1917 (publication: Teresianum, Rome, 1976).

PN   The poems of Thérèse, numbered according to the centenary edition (1979).

PO   *Procès de l'Ordinaire* [bishop's process], 1910–1911 (publication: Teresianum, Rome, 1973).

PST   *The Poetry of Saint Thérèse of Lisieux*. Translated by Donald Kinney, O.C.D. Washington, D.C.: ICS Publications, Institute of Carmelite Studies, 1996.

SS   *Story of a Soul: The Autobiography of St. Thérèse of Lisieux*. Translated by John Clarke, O.C.D. 2d edition. Washington, D.C.: ICS Publications, Institute of Carmelite Studies, 1976.

VT   *Vie thérésienne*, Lisieux (a triennial journal, published since 1961).

When Thérèse of Lisieux
"Irritates" or "Bores"

"Many things in this saint and her writings irritate me or quite simply bore me. And if I set out to explain what nearly nauseates me, so that people would understand it, that still would not account for the fact that I took the trouble to do so. There are so many things in the world to deal with that do not necessitate a long exegesis" (Karl Rahner).[1]

So Thérèse "irritates", "bores", "nauseates" . . . That is clear from what the renowned Jesuit father writes.

Even shortly before the death of Saint Thérèse, one of her companions had said: "My Sister Thérèse of the Child Jesus is going to die soon; and I really wonder what our mother will be able to say after her death. She will be very embarrassed, for this little sister, as likeable as she is, has certainly done nothing worth the trouble of being recounted."[2]

On the other hand, in 1939, Emmanuel Mounier, the founder of the journal *Esprit*, notes:

> We have always experienced some difficulty in the presence of the *petit bourgeois* style in which the heroism of this saint is

---

[1] *Christliche Innerlichkeit* (1973).
[2] HA (1907) 232; cf. PO 177; LC July 29, no. 2, p. 116.

clothed. But each time her life has given us the key of a total detachment. And in a period when the *petit bourgeois* spirit cannot fail to appear as the most dreary antithesis of the Christian life, would it not be a trick of the Holy Spirit, a paradox of Mercy, to have hidden the mysteries of the brightest flame under these banal appearances?

"A trick of the Holy Spirit" . . .

How are we to understand Thérèse of Lisieux?

Do we not still cling to the image of a "stupid nineteenth century"? Of what possible interest is a provincial petite-bourgeoise who enters the cloister? A spirituality inclined to the cult of suffering? An asceticism colored by contempt for or flight from the world? Pious practices anxious to keep an accounting of merits? A prayer apparently unaware of the "collective" or the "political"? A mentality that gives the impression of being victim to the distinction between the earth as a "valley of tears" and heaven, the sole center of interest? Poems of a rather insipid romanticism? Family traumas that would fall as much in the province of psychoanalysis as in that of mysticism? The emotional inflation of a milieu yearning for spiritual revenge, ready to adulterate, censor, slant texts and witnesses in order to obtain a canonization?

Who is Thérèse of Lisieux? The objections are due to ignorance. The game is subtle. One makes up a priori ideas about her in order not to go and see, or else one restricts the reading of her to the prisms of the human sciences alone. After having read and reread for fifty years innumerable works about Thérèse of Lisieux, Julien Green's phrase in *Le Bel Aujourd'hui* comes to mind: "Last night I opened the large volumes by Canon Ribet on mysticism. He was honest enough to tell us, from the very first pages, that he had never experienced any of the things that he was going to describe. In short, he proposed to write a book about China, where he had never set foot, on the basis of works others had written about that country." And Green concludes: "I prefer to go back to Saint Thérèse, who made the voyage herself." Dare we say that the following pages have no other purpose but to open the book of the life and writings of Thérèse of Lisieux in order to invite the reader to that voyage?

Thérèse herself would say: Thérèse is of little importance . . . But what is at stake is one of the most certain and simplest evangelical shortcuts ever proposed.

A trick of the Holy Spirit: Yes, God used and still uses Thérèse of Lisieux. According to my calculations, it would take scarcely half the time to read what is essential in what Thérèse of Lisieux said and wrote as it would to read a long Russian novel! We witness the battle of death and despair with childhood and innocent misfortune, the struggle between darkness and faith, humor and sadness, realism and pretense, maturity and childhood . . . One of the most vivid books in existence is at issue here. Recommended by providence. Contemporary. The life, words, and texts of Thérèse are of an astonishing freshness, accuracy, immediacy, strength, and genius under the "banal appearance".

We should be on our guard: she does not cheat. She poses the most serious and the most unavoidable questions in all life:

Why death? And it is a little girl four years old who asks this question.

How to live in hope to the end? And it is a young girl twenty-four years old who asks this question during eighteen months of agony.

Must we be afraid of the beyond? Can we experience questions in faith?

How to be shaken and yet remain faithful, and do so with joy?

Why suffer if one loves?

And first, how to love?

For one hundred years, Thérèse has been replying.

1897: Jubilee of Queen Victoria

On June 20, 1897, a young eight-year-old British boy, who was to become one of the authorities on the history of the twentieth century, was seated with his father at a window on Fleet Street, London, in order to watch the troops march past in honor of the diamond jubilee of Queen Victoria's reign. He would remember this fifty years later while pondering time and history in some memorable pages. At the same moment, Thérèse of Lisieux, surrounded by the certainty of her death, which she had known to be irreversible for ten days, expressed herself pointedly:

> On June 9, I saw very clearly the beacon that was announcing to me heaven's port; but now I no longer see anything. It's as if my eyes were blindfolded. . . . What anyone says to me about death no longer penetrates; it slides over me as it would over smooth glass. It's finished! The hope of death is all used up. . . . God wills that I abandon myself like a very little child who is not disturbed by what others will do to him. (LC June 15, no. 1, p. 65)

In *Civilization on Trial*, the great historian Arnold J. Toynbee is pondering, then, those days of June 1897, an assessment of the longest reign of the British empire, at the very moment when Thérèse was fighting with death. He writes:

Where does mankind stand . . . ? This question no doubt concerns the whole living generation throughout the world; but, if it were made the subject of a world-wide Gallup Poll, there would be no unanimity in the answer. . . . To whom is our question being addressed? For example, the writer of the present paper is a middle-class Englishman. . . . He knows that his fleeting and fragmentary vision of the passing scene is no more than a caricature of the surveyor's chart. God alone knows the true picture. . . .

The writer's mind runs back fifty years, to an afternoon in London in the year 1897. He is sitting with his father at a window in Fleet Street and watching a procession of Canadian and Australian mounted troops who have come to celebrate Queen Victoria's Diamond Jubilee. He can still remember his excitement at the unfamiliar, picturesque uniforms of these magnificent "colonial" troops, as they were still called in England then: slouch hats instead of brass helmets, grey tunics instead of red. To an English child, this sight gave a sense of new life astir in the world; a philosopher, perhaps, might have reflected that, where there is growth, there is likely also to be decay. . . . The English crowd gazing at that march past of overseas troops in London in 1897 . . . saw their sun standing at its zenith and assumed that it was there to stay. . . . The middle-class English in 1897, who thought of themselves as Wellsian rationalists living in a scientific age, took their imaginary miracle for granted. As they saw it, history, for them, was over. It had come to an end in foreign affairs in 1815, with the Battle of Waterloo; in home affairs in 1832, with the Great Reform Bill; and in imperial affairs in 1859, with the suppression of the Indian Mutiny. And they had every reason to congratulate themselves on the permanent state of felicity which this ending of history had conferred on them. . . . Viewed from the historical vantage point of [fifty years later], this *fin de siècle* middle-class English hallucination seems sheer lunacy, yet it was shared by contemporary Western middle-class people of other nationalities. In the United States, for instance, in the North, history, for the middle class, had come to an end with the winning of the West and the Federal victory in the Civil War; and in Germany, or at any rate in Prussia, for the same class, the same permanent consummation had been reached with the . . . foundation of the Second Reich in 1871. For these three batches of Western middle-class people fifty years ago, God's work of creation was complete, "and behold it was very good."

Toynbee adds:

Yet . . . there were other people abroad who saw things differently—even though they might be impotent and inartic-ulate. . . . There were . . . many people who agreed . . . that history had come to an end. . . . But this sense of finality, which was so gratifying to top dog, did not warm a defeated people's heart. . . . The subterranean movements that could have been detected, even as far back as 1897, by a social seismologist who put his ear to the ground, go far to explain the upheavals and eruptions that have signalized the resump-tion of history's Juggernaut march. . . .[3]

Just after Queen Victoria's jubilee, on June 21, Thérèse would write, in one of her last letters to l'abbé Bellière, then a missionary in Africa:

Like me, you can sing the mercies of the Lord. . . . When I see Magdalene walking up before the many guests, washing with her tears the feet of her adored Master, whom she is touching for the first time, I feel that *her heart* has understood the abysses of love and mercy *of the Heart of Jesus*. . . . Ever since I have been given the grace to understand also the love of the Heart of Jesus, I admit that it has expelled all fear from my heart. . . . When we cast our faults with entire filial

[3] Arnold J. Toynbee, *Civilization on Trial* (New York: Oxford Univ. Press, 1948), pp.16–18, 20.

confidence into the devouring fire of love, how would these not be consumed beyond return? . . . I try to be no longer occupied with myself in anything, and I abandon myself to what Jesus sees fit to do in my soul. (LT 247, GC 2:1133–34)

The pomp of Queen Victoria's jubilee, which gave to one part of the world "the assurance of the definitive", or the hidden fight of Thérèse in her Carmel—history has strange secrets. Faced with the arrival of the barbarians from the north in the fifth century, Saint Jerome had already said: "Everything is lost", while Saint Augustine was proclaiming: "Everything is beginning."

It remains to know how.

1914, 1925, 1973

Three months before the war of 1914, Pope Pius X sought to give Christians a model and said of this young woman that "she is the greatest saint of modern times." She would be beatified nine years later; she would have been fifty years old at the time. She would be canonized two years later, in 1925. Thus, she whose centenary of birth was celebrated in 1973, this *petite bourgeoise* who entered Carmel at fifteen years of age to seek oblivion and self-effacement, was preoccupied with the love of Jesus alone. She died at twenty-four from tuberculosis, as did many young girls in the nineteenth century, yet she would reach millions of people in the world, from Edith Piaf to the last five popes.

The story of the life of Thérèse of Lisieux has gone through eighty-nine editions and has been translated into more than sixty languages (Russian, Chinese, Arabic, Turkish, Swahili, and so on), with five different translations into British and American English. It is, after the Bible, the most widely disseminated religious book in the French language. And from Los Angeles to Ghardaïa, from Beyrouth to Oslo, from Winnipeg to Mexico, surely the most venerated French-woman since the beginning of the twentieth century is found, in her Carmelite habit, with roses in her hand.

PART ONE

HER FACE, HER FAMILY

CHAPTER ONE

Mystic, Comic, Everything

Tall and strong, with the appearance of a child, a tone of voice, an expression, hiding within her a wisdom, a perfection, a perspicacity of a fifty-year-old. . . . Little innocent thing, to whom one would give God without confession, but whose head is full of mischief to play on anyone she pleases. Mystic, comic, everything . . . she can make you weep with devotion and just as easily split your sides with laughter during our recreations. (GC 2:778)

This is the most vivid portrait that has been preserved of her: it was that of her subprioress, when Thérèse was twenty years old. Is that enough to make her "the greatest saint of modern times"?

We have the opportunity to avail ourselves of much testimony about her. In addition to the account of her life that she herself wrote, at twenty-two years of age and completed three months before her death, her sisters, her companions, left a series of interviews, sometimes noted day by day, that retain the sense of immediacy of television news. Through the (apparent) banality of these cartoon strips of piety, we always find the same reality: with Thérèse of Lisieux, we are with someone who, in the face of the two abysses that every man encounters, himself and God, has gone the limit, but while remaining our companion. Thérèse is indeed the human being faced with the abyss of freedom and the possibilities of choice—and faced with another abyss: that of an interlocutor called God (cf. pp. 30–31).

We are still at the dawn of the third great crisis of our civilization: it is no longer merely man confronted with his weakness (with the Greeks); no longer merely man confronted with his guilt (with Luther, at that tragic time for Europe, after the black plagues at the end of the Middle Ages); man today finds himself confronted with his solitude and with the desperate quest for a meaning to his life, confronted with the need to search for what would be an "authentic existence", "true life", which he fears never being able to enjoy. Among the innumerable witnesses that could be called to the stand in this interrogation, such as Rimbaud, Van Gogh, Dostoyevsky, Nietzsche, or Kundera, I have intentionally kept two cries, because they seem to express the question that was Thérèse's own: "Here is my old anguish, right there in the hollow of my body, like a bad wound that every movement irritates; I know its name, it is the fear of eternal solitude. And I have the fear that there may not be any answer" (Camus).

> I implored, I begged for a sign, I sent messages to the heavens: no response. The heavens do not even know my name. I wondered at every moment what I might be in the eyes of God. Now I knew the answer: Nothing. God does not see me, God does not know me, God does not hear me. You see this void over our heads? That is God. You see this hole in the earth? That is God. You see this opening in the door? That is God again. The silence is God. Absence is God. God is the solitude of men.[1]

---

[1] Jean Paul Sartre, *Le Diable et le bon Dieu*, tableau 10, scene 4.

Thérèse was familiar with this anguish:

> When I want to rest my heart fatigued by the darkness
> which surrounds it by the memory of the luminous country
> after which I aspire, my torment redoubles; it seems to me
> that the darkness, borrowing the voice of sinners, says
> mockingly to me: "You are dreaming about the light, about
> a fatherland embalmed in the sweetest perfumes; you are
> dreaming about the *eternal* possession of the Creator of all
> these marvels; you believe that one day you will walk out
> of this fog which surrounds you! Advance, advance; rejoice
> in death which will give you not what you hope for but
> a night still more profound, the night of nothingness."
> (SS 213)

For years, Thérèse sought her place in society. She had, of
course, entered Carmel, but she sought to explain to herself
what the essence of it was for her. And one day, completely
radiant, she wrote:

> *Martyrdom* was the dream of my youth and this dream has
> grown with me within Carmel's cloisters. But here again, I
> feel that my dream is a folly, for I cannot confine myself to
> desiring *one kind* of martyrdom. . . . I opened the Epistles of
> St. Paul to find some kind of answer. Chapters 12 and 13 of
> the First Epistle to the Corinthians fell under my eyes. I
> read there, in the first of these chapters, that *all* cannot be
> apostles, prophets, doctors, etc. . . . The answer . . . did not
> fulfill my desires. . . . I continued my reading, . . . and the
> Apostle explains how all *the most* PERFECT *gifts* are nothing
> without LOVE. . . .
>
> I finally had rest. . . . I understood that LOVE COMPRISED
> ALL VOCATIONS, THAT LOVE WAS EVERYTHING, THAT IT EM-
> BRACED ALL TIMES AND ALL PLACES. . . .
>
> Then, in the excess of my delirious joy, I cried out: . . . MY
> VOCATION IS LOVE!" (SS 193–94)

She had chosen the feast of Pentecost 1887 to confide to her father her desire to enter Carmel:

> Everything around us corresponded with our tastes; we were given the greatest liberty; I would say our life on earth was *the ideal of happiness*. . . . It was necessary to turn away from it freely. . . . I chose the *feast of Pentecost* . . . , all day long begging the apostles to pray for me, to inspire me with the right words. Shouldn't they help the timid child who was chosen by God to be the apostle of the apostles through her prayers and sacrifices? . . . (SS 106–7)

Her father was convinced. But the others remained . . . And the trip to Rome would still not win the victory. Here is how she described her interview with the pope:

> God is making me pass through real trials before having me enter Carmel. I am going to tell you how my visit with the pope went. . . . I did not want to return to my place without having spoken to the pope. I said what you were telling me in your letter. . . . The good pope is so old that one would say he is dead. . . . He can hardly say anything. . . . I would have liked to be able to explain my business, but there was no way. The Holy Father said simply: "If God wills it, you will enter." (LT 36, GC 1:353)

She would have to wait. Finally, everyone would be won over by the one who admitted: "I haven't any fear of anyone; I have always gone where I pleased. I always slipped by them" (LC July 10, no. 8, p. 85).

A "trick of the Holy Spirit". That is the primary statement of fact. Thérèse of Lisieux, beneath the appearance of a very nice little girl, is a soldier, a warrior. She is the equal of the greatest among the giants God has recommended to us, but under the most banal exterior.

In April 1932, during a private audience with Bishop
Picaud of Bayeux and Lisieux, Pius XI thought that the
image of Thérèse was in the process of being watered down,
and at that time he used the expression "a great man" to
describe her.[2] The bishop reported this to the Carmel. Which
was a bit of a shock to her sisters, for whom Thérèse still
remained a "little angel". But it was quite in these terms that
Thérèse had spoken of herself: "armed for war", taking up
the call of Teresa of Avila to her daughters to "equal strong
men" (cf. LT 201, GC 2:1016–17).

She brought about a revolution. We are only at the beginning of it.

She passed through the door of Carmel at fifteen and a half
years of age. Now, Carmel is far from being "heaven". And
she admitted:

> Nothing near Jesus. Aridity! . . . Sleep! . . . But at least there
> is silence! . . . I would be unhappy possessing [all created
> beauties], my heart would be so empty! . . . It is incredible
> how big my heart appears to me when I consider all earth's
> treasures. But when I consider Jesus, how little it appears to
> me! . . . I would so much like to love Him! . . . Love Him
> more than He has ever been loved! (LT 74, GC 1:499–500)

In Carmel, there was solitude, a life of penitence, one meal
per day, seven months out of twelve; little, too little, sleep;
cold (a single room was heated); the experience of life with
those one did not choose; the daily pinpricks. She noted with
a smile: "The refectory, which I was given charge of immediately after I received the Habit, furnished me, on more than
one occasion, with the chance of putting my self-love in its
proper place, i.e., under my feet" (SS160).

[2] Cf. *La Semaine religieuse de Bayeux*, May 1, 1932; reprinted in *La Croix* of
May 18, 1932.

A Warrior

She did not allow herself to weaken: "My nature was such that fear made me recoil; with *love*, not only did I advance, I actually *flew*" (SS 174).

> I have experienced it; when I *am feeling* nothing, when I am INCAPABLE *of praying*, of practicing virtue, then is the moment for seeking opportunities, *nothings*, which please Jesus more than mastery of the world or even martyrdom suffered with generosity. For example, a smile, a friendly word, when I would want to say nothing, or put on a look of annoyance. (LT 143, GC 2:801)

To understand her secret as a warrior, we might go back to Nehru's admission to Malraux: "I have three enemies: the Chinese, famine, and myself. But, of the three, the most difficult is myself." Very quickly she learned that nothing can be done on the path of what for her was the true life without fighting against herself, against illusion. She, who, up to the end, had the childish fears of a little girl, would never fear the truth, never fear to "do the truth", as Saint John says: whether about herself, her faults, her own limits, about her family, her community, her sisters, or one day about death itself. She did not fear that the truth would diminish her. Quite the contrary. It was never a malicious truth. For she found here the true way to be victorious: by disarming, by never resisting. Instead of sidestepping an issue, cheating, trying to justify herself, telling herself stories, she disarmed, and she disarmed from the very moment when the truth was at issue. Then she found something greater: a confidence that opened up freedom to her.

Her sister Céline, older than she, who entered Carmel six years after she did, reported that one day, in watching Thérèse

live, she experienced a moment of discouragement and said
to her: "Oh, when I think of all I have to acquire." And
Thérèse answered her at once: "Rather, how much you have
to lose" (CSG 23).

> As the novices used to ask her how they should conduct
> themselves when it came to spiritual direction, Thérèse re-
> plied: "With great simplicity, but without relying too much
> on help that might fail the minute you put it into practice.
> You would quickly be forced to say, like the spouse in the
> Song of Songs: 'The watchmen . . . took away my mantle,
> they wounded me; it was only by passing a little beyond them
> that I found Him whom I love' [cf. Song 5:7; 3:4]. If you ask
> the watchmen humbly and with detachment where your Be-
> loved is, they will tell you. Nevertheless, most often you will
> find Jesus only after you have passed beyond all creatures."
> (PO 369 r°/v°)

*

What in former times was reserved to privileged souls—Bernard of Cîteaux, Ignatius of Loyola, or John of the Cross—we
find Thérèse of Lisieux proposing for everyone: to triumph
over the agony of her fate, to triumph over fear and solitude
in the face of the uncertainties of the future and of death.
Thérèse gives away the secrets of this "democratization" of
the "night of the spirit". For her, there is in each one of us an
infinite, explosive power that can conquer all fear. Thérèse is
in agreement with the prophets and the great revolutionaries
of her time who were seeking this power: this power exists, it
is in each one of us. It is possible to conquer fear, all fear: that
of the future, that of limits, that of others, that of death, of
oneself. There is one condition for enjoying this infinite
power: accepting the truth about one's incapacity.

It was fitting that, before the last council gave more explicit recognition to the place of the laity and theorized about it, the Church had first been anticipated, even shoved forward, by this little girl. A priest from Vietnam wrote:

> The centennial year of Saint Thérèse's birth occurs even here among the most distant. Here, Dalat, tribus Kohos, primitive tribes of the high plains. The mountain people of this region are haunted by fear, fear of spirits. Their worship is centered on the blood of beasts to appease the anger of the spirits. Say to God: "Our Father"? Consecrate oneself to his love? What a revolution! May this year bring to our companions the tenderness of heaven. Here, the spirit of the sun is called Siet Ngkao ("Cut-off-the-head"); the spirit of the rainbow: Jop Mham ("Suck-the-blood", like vampires); the spirit of thunder: Cong Co ("Cut-with-the-axe"); the spirit of water: Kuansan ("Claw-and-eat") . . . And so on for the others: always *against* man. At last, Thérèse will speak to them of a God who is *for* man.

"Cut-off-the-head", "Suck-the-blood", "Claw-and-eat". Who is without his evil spirits, and who has no need of being delivered from fear?

CHAPTER TWO

A Few Landmarks

A Young Girl Is Converted

Being the youngest in the family, I wasn't accustomed to doing things for myself. Céline tidied up the room in which we slept, and I myself didn't do any housework whatsoever. . . . I was really unbearable because of my extreme touchiness; if I happened to cause anyone I loved some little trouble, even unwittingly, instead of forgetting about it and not *crying*, which made matters worse, I *cried* like a Magdalene and then when I began to cheer up, I'd begin *to cry again for having cried*. All arguments were useless. . . . I really don't know how I could entertain the thought of entering Carmel when I was still in the *swaddling clothes of a child*!

God would have to work a little miracle to make me *grow up* in an instant, and this miracle He performed on that unforgettable Christmas Day. . . .

It was December 25, 1886, that I received . . . the grace of my complete conversion. We had come back from Midnight Mass. . . . Upon arriving at Les Buissonnets, I used to love to take my shoes from the chimney-corner. . . . [*The one who is speaking would turn fourteen several days later.*] [Jesus] permitted Papa, tired out after the Midnight Mass, to experience annoyance when seeing my shoes at the fireplace, and that he speak those words which pierced my heart: "Well,

fortunately, this will be the last year! . . ." I was going up-
stairs, at the time, to remove my hat, and Céline, knowing
how sensitive I was and seeing the tears already glistening
in my eyes, . . . said: "Oh, Thérèse, don't go downstairs; it
would cause you too much grief to look at your slippers
right now!" But Thérèse was no longer the same; Jesus had
changed her heart! Forcing back my tears, I descended the
stairs rapidly; controlling the poundings of my heart, I took
my slippers and placed them in front of Papa, and withdrew
all the objects joyfully. I had the happy appearance of a
Queen. Having regained his own cheerfulness, Papa was
laughing; Céline believed it was all a *dream*! . . .

On that *night of light* began the third period of my life, the
most beautiful and the most filled with graces from heaven.
The work I had been unable to do in ten years was done by
Jesus in one instant. (SS 97–98)

When did she write these lines, and who is she? Who are her
contemporaries? A few landmarks will allow us to situate her.

She wrote down the story of her conversion in the period
when Rimbaud published *A Season in Hell*, a text that gave an
account of the despair that had periodically filled humanity
for a century. It was the time when Dostoyevsky's *The Possessed* was published; when the philosopher Nietzsche expressed his distress in his book *Human, All Too Human*.

Four crises were shaking society at that time: (1) the post-
war period of 1870; (2) the end of a council (we know that
that is never easy); (3) a new confrontation between Catholics
and politics on the occasion of the birth of a republic; and (4)
a tense renewal of the debate between science and faith. It
was in 1878 that Claude Bernard would publish the charter of
all modern science with his book *La Science expérimentale*.

These are the events that this nineteenth century, drawing
to a close, calls to mind at the very moment when Thérèse

confirmed her vocation with one stroke by her "Christmas conversion". She was thirteen and a half years old. Doctor Freud, the inventor of psychoanalysis, was working at Charcot's and just glimpsing the broad outlines of what would become Freudianism. The first theory of psychoanalysis dates from one year before Thérèse's death. Marx would die three years before Thérèse. That same year, 1886, Nietzsche would also publish *Beyond Good and Evil*. And he was preparing the publication of *The Antichrist*, which would come out the year Thérèse entered Carmel. Claudel's conversion took place on exactly the same day as that of Thérèse of Lisieux; Charles de Foucauld's, three months earlier. It was the year when Van Gogh, after his stay in Paris, left for Arles. Wagner, after having written *Parsifal* (1877–1882), had just broken with the revolutionary prophet of despair and revolt, his friend the philosopher Nietzsche. The latter wrote to Wagner: "Hell! You yourself have collapsed before the Cross! You too! You too! You defeated man, you have fallen to your knees."

The same day as Thérèse's "conversion", December 25, 1886, would see the publication of the *Confessions d'un libre penseur* (Confessions of a freethinker), by Léo Taxil, an impostor whose story would mark her personally. Marx, Nietzsche, Freud: three giants who dominate modern thought—roses are no longer in question here . . . Yet, it is only in the company of these three that we must dare to speak of Thérèse of Lisieux today, for the same battle is at issue: man in the face of his abysses. Thérèse was definitely one of those who went the farthest, "all the way to the end". When she chose the good, she knew—and she said so—what it would have been for her to choose rupture, solitude, and evil; and when she pursued the search for her God, she knew that it was not first of all she who was seeking but that it was he who sought her: "He will more quickly grow tired of making me wait than I shall grow tired of waiting for Him!" (LT 103, GC 1:612).

*

Thérèse probably did not even know of the existence of her contemporary the philosopher Nietzsche. But the parallel that can now be established is highly revealing. In fact, Thérèse would be pursued by the same fear that haunted the great prophets of modernity: How does one respond to the violence of the desire that dwells in human beings? How does one find liberation and freedom? Is it necessary to follow the intoxication of Nietzsche and say: No more interlocutors, no more limits, and proclaim the death of God? Or, with Thérèse, to go all the way to the end of the night in order to trust? Nietzsche professed to be the prophet of the will to power, of the exclusion of all dogmatisms and all moralisms. The death of God would finally be proclaimed if one managed to establish the death of the idea of God in the West. Nietzsche questioned and proclaimed: "Where is God? I am going to tell you. We have killed him, you and I. We are all murderers. Don't you feel the breath of emptiness over you? Hasn't everything become colder? Hasn't the night arrived, ever more the night? Gods decay, too. God is dead. God will stay dead." [1] Which did not prevent Nietzsche from repeating: "The most painful, the most agonizing question is that of the heart that wonders: Where could I feel at home?" Nietzsche professed to be the prophet of the most "innocent", childlike affirmation possible. One need only refer to his evocation of the threefold metamorphosis that he conjures up in *Thus Spake Zarathustra* (that of the camel, the lion,

[1] *The Gay Science*, 1882, bk. 3, § 125.

and the child), the transfiguration finally obtained of human freedom carried to the extreme of sincerity: the desire to be God that is inscribed in freedom can, for him, be realized only through the absolute refusal of any possibility of a "supernatural" gift. For Nietzsche, to accept anything else would amount to admitting a rival to man. Now, to be free, one must definitively eliminate any rival.

Starting with the same question, that of freedom, Thérèse of Lisieux takes another path. She is the prophet of the will to weakness, if we might dare put it that way. Of course, she is also the prophet of liberation from all narrow moralism, all self-satisfaction, all pride in being righteous by one's own power. But God is no longer competitive; he is, on the contrary, the ultimate accomplice of our fragility itself. And this, too, comes in the most "innocent", the most "childlike" affirmation possible. She is indeed the prophet of human freedom, but brought down to the greatest depths of humility. For Thérèse, this desire for God that constitutes our freedom can be realized only through the total, radical, acceptance of the gift, which is itself radical, that God makes of his "power" to our weakness. Thérèse knows what she is saying when she reveals her secret: "God could not inspire unattainable desires."

The "Persecution Case"

Thérèse was born on January 2, 1873. When she was only six years old, in June 1879, there was the bill against religious teaching orders. In March 1880 there were the anticlerical decrees in France and the dissolution of the Society of Jesus. Can we imagine what the suppression of the Jesuit order would mean today? That same year, when she was seven years old, 261 convents were closed in France. An authorization was required within three months for the maintenance of any congregation. Then came the first wave of expulsions. We still have numerous accounts of it, for example, concerning the Dominican house of studies at Flavigny, in Burgundy, where the first companions of Father Lacordaire are buried, or in the memories of families in the village of Solesmes who took in the monks chased from their monastery.

The following year, on October 3, 1881, Thérèse, at the age of eight, entered the boarding school of the Benedictines of Lisieux. The next year, on March 28, 1882, the anticlerical laws were passed in France as well as the prohibition of giving religious instruction on scholastic premises. For a little girl, what sudden changes! Thérèse's family and childhood were hardly spared.

In 1894, when the first centenary was celebrated of the martyrdom of the Carmelites of Compiègne, who were guillotined under the Terror, the Lisieux Carmel was given the task of making the decorative banners for it, and Thérèse participated in this with fervor. That same year the so-called *scélérate* [wicked] laws were enacted in France. The Lisieux Carmelites were going to have permanently under their straw mattresses a little box called the "persecution case" in which a few civilian clothes were put away in case they should have to leave quickly. It was the year Joan of Arc was proclaimed venerable. It is understandable that Joan's figure had a profound effect on Thérèse, who prayed for her beatification. The photograph of Thérèse dressed as Joan of Arc for a recreation in Carmel is well known. It was this very photograph that the Carmel, in its naïveté, would send to the impostor Léo Taxil. The latter would show it with his projector in the great hall of the Geographical Society on the boulevard Saint-Germain in Paris, at a press conference during which he unveiled his hoax and, by implication, the stupidity of the Lisieux Carmelites, whom he, the anticlerical agnostic, had urged to pray for the conversion of someone who did not exist: Diana Vaughan. Thérèse would be upset by this. She would erase and scratch out their names in the recreation text entitled *The Triumph of Humility* and would go to tear up the letters of Léo Taxil over the manure heap at the back of the garden in the Carmel, after having asked her sisters never to speak of it again.

Members and Ambience of the Family

Before understanding the ambience—one would readily say the "music of the soul"—of Thérèse's family, let us recall something about its members.

Her family had both a peasant and a military ancestry. It was not for nothing that Thérèse would be both a warrior and a realist. Her father followed the travels of his own father, from garrison to garrison—Avignon, Strasbourg—he grew up in military camps. He was a meticulous, precise man with an artist's temperament. He loved his work of clock and watchmaking. He thought about entering religious life, and he presented himself at the monastery of Grand-Saint-Bernard. He was not accepted because he did not know Latin.

Thérèse's mother, Zélie Guérin, lively, intelligent, full of good sense, courageous, received a very good convent education. She won a first prize for style. We find that again in the vivacity of her correspondence. She also wanted to be a religious, with the Sisters of Saint Vincent de Paul, at the Hôtel Dieu in Alençon. She presented herself there with her mother, and there she was as easily refused by the superior as Louis Martin had been by the father abbot of Grand-Saint-Bernard. So we cannot forget that with both parents there was a religious vocation as well as realism. Zélie began "point Alençon", a special lace famous in that city, and with the help of her sister set up a business on her own.

He was thirty-five, she was twenty-seven when they married, on July 13, 1858. Now, a rather impressive fact, the two decided to live as brother and sister. At the end of ten months, their confessor intervened and reminded them that marriage has a different purpose. This confessor was so well understood that they would have nine children. In 1870, the father quit clock-making (he was forty-seven years old) in order to look after the business affairs of his wife, who was a relentless worker. She made a good living, but she had one obsession: to provide for what her children would need, for life would not be so easy nor the future assured. It is enough, for example, to recall that in 1870 nine German soldiers would live at their house.

The family atmosphere was not sad. It was that of happy music. Prayer held an essential place. The rhythm of their life was governed by the liturgy, guided by a real abandonment to the divine will. They would not have worked on Sundays for all the gold in the world. They did not work even when the work was urgent. The family was not wealthy. The Jansenist climate common at that time was not experienced there. They were not merely regular churchgoers. The Martin parents rose every morning at 5:30 to go to Mass, which was not the usual custom. They received Communion frequently, which was rare at that time. Religion did not remain theoretical or abstract. The poor were truly God's representatives and were effectively helped: there were old people whom they looked after, helped out, housed; the dying were visited by Mme. Martin; at the risk of contagion, she cared for those who lived on her street.

Children arrived. Each had his own character.

Marie was the eldest, independent, nonconformist, quite original. As an adolescent, she did not want either to marry or to be a religious when asked what she would be.

Pauline, the second oldest, was the confidante and favorite of her mother. She was intelligent, resourceful. She was called the boy of the family. She was energetic and gifted. She would become prioress at the Carmel.

Léonie, who was invariably called "poor Léonie", was like the ugly duckling of the family, not very gifted, often sick, the only one to concern her mother. She would become a Visitandine Sister in Mans.

Céline, the clever, fearless one, was the inseparable companion of Thérèse.

Let us not forget little Hélène, dead at five and one-half years, who was very beautiful and whose death would be very difficult, especially for M. Martin.

And then Thérèse came, into a climate of joy and intense family life. The atmosphere was happy. There were games, songs. The father loved to sing, and Thérèse had an amazing, formidable gift for imitating. Outings to the countryside, family trips, evenings; a great taste for pilgrimages, pantomime, and M. Martin made toys for his daughters. On December 15, 1872, Thérèse's mother, who loved life passionately, wrote: "I am madly in love with children; I was born to have them, but it will soon be time for this to end. I shall be forty-one years old on the twenty-third of this month; this is an age when one is a grandmother!" (GC 2:1199).

Thérèse was born January 2, 1873, several days after this letter.

CHAPTER THREE

Before Carmel: Three Trials, Three Blessings

THREE TRIALS

1. *The Death of Four Brothers and Sisters*

The happy atmosphere of this life, nonetheless, went through severe grief with the death of four children.

The eldest, Marie, was born in 1860; then Pauline in 1861; Léonie in 1863; a little Hélène would be born in 1864 who, as we said, died at five and a half years; then the birth of Louis in 1866, a little boy who would die at five months; in 1867, Jean-Baptiste, who would die at eight months. In April 1868, there was the birth of Céline; then, in 1870, a little Thérèse, who would die at the age of two months. Which makes very understandable Mme. Martin's anxiety as the birth of Thérèse drew near in January 1873.

Two boys and seven girls, but four of them dead at a young age, to say nothing of the death, at the same time, of four members of the immediate family, including three of the grandparents. Even though Mme. Martin had a passion for life, one of the recent biographers of Thérèse of Lisieux had the audacity to mention these deaths while implying that Mme. Martin wished to have children only in order to send them to heaven, and he called her a "maker of angels". I, in fact, can confirm the truth of this situation on the basis of my own family. My grandmother, who was married shortly after Mme. Martin, lost exactly the same number of children at an early age. The Martin family experienced what was unfortunately the normal rate of infant mortality at that time, even in comparatively well-cared-for families.

2. *The Death of Thérèse's Mother*

At the end of December 1876, Mme. Martin consulted a doctor, who spoke candidly with her. His frankness left her no hope: it was serious; an operation on this "fibrous tumor", which today we would call a cancer, would be useless. There was dismay in the family. Mme. Martin wrote: "I am grateful to the doctor for his frankness, for I am going to lose no time in settling my affairs so as not to leave my family in difficulty." As for the operation, it was too late. She hid her pain by trying to be cheerful. Marie could not get over the heroism she showed in going to Mass: "Mama still wanted to go to early Mass, but it required extraordinary courage and effort in order to get to the church." She went on pilgrimage to Lourdes. During the three days spent there, she plunged four times into the icy water of the baths. She had two months left to live.

And Thérèse? Can we imagine what the courage of her mother represented for her when she, in her turn, would experience eighteen months of tubercular agony? Perhaps insufficient note has been taken of the obvious role of this memory, quite probably very present to Thérèse, of the unrelenting strength of her mother before her death. As Thérèse herself writes, she remembered the illness and burial of her mother. She records with great specificity: "All the details of my Mother's illness are still present to me and I recall especially the last weeks she spent on earth. Céline and I were like two poor little exiles, for every morning, Mme. Leriche came to get us" (SS 33). She never forgot the ceremony of Extreme Unction: "I still see the spot where I was by Céline's side" (SS 33). Mme. Martin died in August 1877. She was not yet forty-six years old. "Once", writes Thérèse, "I was standing before the lid of the coffin. . . . I stopped for a long time gazing at it. Though I'd never seen one before, I understood what it was. I was so little that in spite of Mamma's small stature, I had to *raise* my head to take in its full height. It appeared *large* and *dismal*" (SS 34).

M. Martin left Alençon with his children in order to be nearer his wife's family by settling in Lisieux, where Uncle Guérin, his brother-in-law, was a pharmacist. He had to organize his life differently. Nothing, ever, would be the same as before. Thérèse left Alençon, where she had been very happy. She would return there only six years later.

3. *The Departure of Sisters for Carmel*

Thérèse lived through this bereavement twice. It was the third shock of her family life. She went through it a first time at the departure for Carmel of her second sister, Pauline, the one she had chosen to replace her mother. She learned of this decision by chance, which upset her even more. But instead of feeling dread or tension with regard to Carmel, on the contrary, it made her love Carmelite life. She wrote with surprising lucidity: "It was not the dream of a child led astray but the *certitude* of a divine call; I wanted to go to Carmel not for *Pauline's sake* but for *Jesus alone*" (SS 58). The mother prioress took seriously the vocation of little Thérèse, who was only nine years old at the time. That did not prevent Thérèse from feeling the moments spent in the parlor of

Carmel as torture, for she was entitled only to two or three minutes at the end of a conversation measured by a half-hour timer. Pauline herself, who had become Sister Agnès in Carmel, would perceive this only later: "If I had known what she was capable of suffering in those parlor visits."

Thérèse's sensitive nature could not withstand it. She became profoundly ill at the age of ten years. Certainly, she had always been overly tearful and excessively emotional, but this was a matter of a more severe anxiety. The doctors were stumped; the diagnosis was vague: "a very grave illness to which no child has been subject". They prescribed hydrotherapy. Her father, who was in Paris, was called back by telegram. He was dismayed. The illness became so serious that, humanly speaking, they thought Thérèse was going to die. Her father wondered if his poor little daughter, who resembled an idiot, was to die or to remain in that state for the rest of her life.

And there was the cure by the smile of the statue of the Virgin. A novena had been made in the Carmel. The family statue of Our Lady of Victories had been placed in Thérèse's room. Thérèse recovered when she saw the Virgin smile at her. Certainly a cure, but soon followed by a still more serious relapse. Thérèse had in fact promised herself not to speak of this exceptional grace. But her sister Marie pressed her so urgently that she spoke and at the same instant fell back into her scruples. Her culpability increased. She who had promised to keep the secret felt she had betrayed it.

Then there was a second departure for Carmel, that of her older sister Marie. Again, Thérèse, who was then thirteen and a half years old, had a relapse. It was like the loss of her third mother. It is easy to understand why Thérèse would write of this time that preceded her conversion: "I was really unbearable because of my extreme touchiness" (SS 97).

If we had to make a prognosis, we could say with justification that "nothing looked promising." Everything was set to end in failure: a hard, ultimately deadly political climate; a family dislocated by the death of the mother, who had been its strongest component; a vocation that could seem ambiguous. Now Thérèse transformed, reversed, converted everything, not by heroism or aggressiveness, but by the confidence and determination to follow her "little way". Her faith, lived like the most beautiful fruit of love, was going to become a force for conversion in the face of weakness and fragility. Prayer and fidelity to the presence of Jesus were going to become the secret for mastering a weakened sensitivity, not only by resoluteness but by trust. And the family presence of her sisters was going to become one of the finest successes of the communion of saints.

THREE BLESSINGS

1. *The Faith of Her Parents*

Thérèse's family suffered adversities. A strange, persistent tendency, both revanchist and recurring, regularly strives to run down the members of it with analytical psychology or apparently well-founded historical science. Father Conrad De Meester, Father Descouvemont, Bishop Guy Gaucher, Sister Cécile, and Sister Geneviève, following Fathers François de Sainte-Marie, Victor Sion, and Bishop Combes, have provided everything that is necessary to anyone wishing to be honest. No one in Thérèse's family needs to be rehabilitated. "Heaven" has taken care of it for one hundred years, is taking care of it now, and will continue to do so. No truth need be feared here. Nor are we forbidden to note three blessings that Thérèse was able to draw from her family context.

First of all, the faith of her father. We should be more precise. It is not merely a question of the passing, albeit profound, desires for religious life on the part of both her parents, nor even of their exceptional wish to live out their marriage commitment in chastity, but really first of all it was a question of fidelity to a life of habitual, happy prayer whose rhythm was set by the Church's feast days and which was lived with a heroic persistence by Mme. Martin up to the time when her death drew near. We might add, too, the strength of their trust and abandonment to providence in a right balance between a piety tailored to cater to personal preferences, or even ostentatious or less than rigorous, and a strict Jansenism. It was neither one nor the other. Thérèse received from this family balance an image of God that would have immense consequences of immeasurable importance. Cardinal Congar compared it to that of an atomic explosion, at the beginning of this century, destined to free the Church of the weight of Jansenism and stoicism, which had burdened spirits for centuries. It is evident that Thérèse owed her image of God in large part to the intelligent, strong, and knowing tenderness, ever-present but without indulgence, that her father had for her and that she had for her father. John Paul II summed this up very well in his homily at the basilica during his visit to Lisieux in 1980: "The Spirit of God permitted her heart to reveal directly to the men of our time the fundamental mystery, the gospel reality: God is our Father, and we are his children." This would certainly be a principal justification for declaring Thérèse a Doctor of the Church.[1] There is no question the Holy Father had good reason to recognize her parents as deserving the title "venerable", the starting point

---

[1] Thérèse was in fact officially declared Doctor of the Church by Pope John Paul II in Rome on October 19, 1997, one year after the original publication of this book in French.—TRANS.

for recognizing an authentic holiness. We will examine later the grace with which Thérèse transmitted a theologically very sound idea of the twofold movement of thought needed by all the faithful in order to respect the paternity proper to the Christian God.

2. *The Realism of Her Mother*

If the firm, simple, and profound affection that existed between Thérèse and her father helped her to situate herself in a true and theological manner before God, Thérèse owed a second blessing to her mother. The latter was incontestably the mainspring of the family. We know her love of life, her organizational skills, her respect of persons, for example, in relation to their family servant, and very obviously her courage in the face of the tragic death of four children. Like her mother, Thérèse would be surprisingly strong and realistic. In a word, we could call this Norman realism, but we should immediately add: without "pretense", to use her own expression, or aggressiveness; which is not so banal in context, a fortiori in the unbelievable struggle of her illness, accurately depicted by the medical treatments to which she had to submit.

Instead of attacking her mother and sisters (as certain biographers do), it would perhaps be more fruitful to reverse the perspective and ask the true questions. For example, if Thérèse retained so precise a memory of the illness and confrontation with death that her mother experienced, it would be surprising if she did not think back on this again, even if she did not speak about it very much at the time, when she herself experienced the clear beginning of her illness. In fact, more than three and a half months passed between the moment when she was told she was in danger of not surviving the night (on June 9) and the day of her death (September 30).

To the example of her mother could be added that of her sisters. We know that Pauline took no special precaution to spare Thérèse's sensibilities when she decided to leave home to enter Carmel. Of course, it is surprising to find that Thérèse did not take part in household work and, what seems quite unbelievable today, had never even washed dishes before entering Carmel. But precisely the flexibility, speed, and cleverness with which she adapted to Carmel proved, if necessary, the formidable capacity for attention to practical reality that she received from her mother and shared with her sisters.

It is not enough to note this in passing. We must add that this, like her sense of the divine paternity, is one of the very particular aspects of her genius. Jean Guitton was right to note that the saints have usually preferred heaven to earth, while, for Thérèse, it was the opposite. We have here, indeed, something original. It is also one of the notes that was to be emphasized in naming her a Doctor of the Church. Thérèse gave full value to the concrete, to everyday concerns, to the seriousness of what we have to do on earth, to the patience required by time, to the "little nothings", but once again, without abruptness, with gentleness, without tension, without violence. Her understanding of reality illustrates well what Saint Thomas Aquinas says of the virtue of fortitude when he recalls that this virtue has two components: combativeness (*aggredi*) and the ability "to stand fast" (*sustinere*), and that "to stand fast" is the more important. All the letters to Céline, like all the advice to her novices, prove that Thérèse understood perfectly what that meant, for instance, during the passion of the final eighteen months, just as she had "stood fast" through the fortitude of silence during the illness of her father. She had a sense of the value of the temporal, of the value of the present, of the importance of the least daily tasks. That was important for her. She liked the present, and she said: "I do not really see what more I would have in heaven than I have right now. I will see God, it is true; but as for being with him, I am already totally with him on earth" (PA 409). For her, time was the only means by which we can respond to God by proving to him our trust and by giving him our freedom.

3. *A Right Sense of the Realities of the Heart*

A third blessing certainly came to her from the climate of heart in which the family lived. We discern there no pointless settling of accounts, no retrospective discontent, no tension, bitterness, jealousy. We find an affection normally expressed with joy, with happiness, during feast days, sittings for photographs, little plays and recreation. In a word, the heart was in its proper place. The letters of Thérèse's mother when pregnant with her children, like the correspondence of Céline and Léonie addressed to their cloistered sisters in Carmel when they were caring for their ill father, transcribe with sufficient truth the normal anxieties, affectionate concern, or delicate attentions of beings who were struggling against death or who were crushed by the confinement of their father. With paternal trust and maternal realism, the equilibrium of heart among the sisters was a new blessing for the communion of saints.

CHAPTER FOUR

In Carmel: Three Trials, Three Blessings

THREE TRIALS

1. *The State and Composition of the Community*

The presence of five members of the same family (four sisters and one cousin) among twenty-two Carmelites and two extern Sisters would be formidable for any community. There is the obvious risk of their forming a clique, not to speak of a lump! On any occasion a little group could form that would become a leading or an opposing force. How many communities have almost failed to resist this, or have not resisted it?

This was especially true in Lisieux, since it is clear that on certain points the rule was not very well followed there. The example often cited was the inclination to fail in silence in Thérèse's community. The Sisters had a tendency to forget this rule of silence—though strict in the monasteries of this period—in the places where they lived their regular life in common. They had gotten into the habit of gathering in the cloisters to exchange news from the city after a parlor visit. What did Thérèse do? Not sit in judgment. One witness says merely: "She took no interest in news or conversations when

45

the rule of charity did not make it a duty for her. The little gatherings that one so often saw left her indifferent. She passed by them without stopping and recommended that her novices not lose time in listening to those sorts of talk that did not concern them" (Sister Thérèse of Saint Augustine, PA 335–36). Thérèse's bearing and posture were so characteristic that the gardener of the monastery was able to recognize her from her gait alone, despite the great veil, which, according to the custom of the Carmel, she wore covering her face when an outsider was inside enclosure. This observance of silence is one of the most important obligations in the life of Carmelites (cf. chapter 16, "The Power of Silence"). It is given the form of a precept in the primitive rule (no. 18). Teresa of Avila, the foundress of the reformed Carmel, went back to it in her constitutions (no. 7) and commented on it in her writings. The *Papier d'exaction*, a kind of custom book that took up the requirements, the degree of "correctness", to which the Carmelites were to be held and of which Thérèse had a copy, as did each of her Sisters, also insists on it. Thérèse's attention to this point would go so far that witnesses often repeated that she forced herself not to seek the society of her three sisters, despite the very lively affection she bore them (cf. VT 75 [1979]: 231; VT 99 [1985]:176; PO 37; PA 1187; CG 2:648).

That does not mean to say that life at the Carmel was not rigorous. It was in Lisieux. Five and a half hours of sleep in the summer—Thérèse would suffer from it and would fall asleep at prayer (which earned us, we may add, one of the finest remarks in the history of spirituality on the life of prayer). But Thérèse never went beyond her own role in order to bring back to the rule what rightly seemed to her deficient. On the contrary, she would herself follow the constitutions with redoubled attention.

One other stumbling block stemming from the composition of the Carmel has been noted. There were few young novices at the time Thérèse entered. The age difference might have led to affective preferences and risked making her a little pet. Thérèse understood this very well and explicitly praised the wisdom of Mother Marie de Gonzague, her prioress, on that account.

2. The Temperament of the Mother Prioress

People have often tried to account for the holiness of Thérèse of Lisieux by placing her "against" someone.[1] The novelist Van der Meersch tried to explain Thérèse's grace "against" her prioress. Recently, other biographers have worked desperately hard to interpret Thérèse's grace "against" the morbid state of her parents or the a priori insipidness of her sisters. There is no need to be "against" anyone in order to understand and venerate the holiness of Thérèse, beginning with her mother prioress. If the history of the relationship between Thérèse and the latter is one of the principal tasks of future Thérèsian studies (cf. NEC, Ms A 69 v° 8, p. 214 n. and 70 v°, p. 218 n. [SS 148–49]), several simple and true points remain nonetheless assured. A deep, fine, and noble affection existed between Thérèse and her prioress. They grasped the greatness and the opportunity of the tasks that were given to them mutually: in the prioress, despite the limits we shall discuss, the importance and stakes of a psychological and spiritual discernment; in Thérèse, the decisive place of an intelligent obedience and espousing the intention of the superior.

Mother Marie de Gonzague had a strong temperament.

---

[1] See, at the end of the volume, appendix 2, entitled "Thérèse of Lisieux, Joan of Arc, and the Mystics", pp. 245ff.

Her face did not have a very gracious look to it. Certain photographs give witness to it. One day when a novice of Saint Thérèse had given the prioress the nickname of "the wolf", Thérèse said nothing. It was well observed. Thérèse's instinct for comic imitation persuaded her that it might be dangerous for such a nickname to be attached to her prioress. She cut the matter short (cf. Sister Marie of the Trinity, PA 1219 and PO 1069 r°).

Of aristocratic origin, Mother Marie de Gonzague could at times be tempted to make use of this when, for example, she asked certain Sisters to go keep her own mother company in the parlor, obviously against the rule.

One detail from the canonization process will suffice. Following an objection from one of the Roman censors, who had thought to see in Thérèse's attitude a lack of deference toward authority, the judge of the process asked a witness, Sister Aimée of Jesus, for more details. He would have the episode confirmed by two other witnesses, one of whom was a sister of Thérèse. He wanted to know if she was always even-tempered with Mother Marie de Gonzague. The latter was at the time no longer prioress but subprioress and novice mistress.

Here is the account of the episode as reported by Mother Agnès, sister of Saint Thérèse, in the canonization process:

It was during the month of January 1896; I was prioress and had to remain in that office until February 20. My sister Céline [the last to enter Carmel, since she had taken care of her father during the three years of his illness] was coming to the end of her novitiate year. She could be admitted to profession on February 6. So there was the question of presenting her to the chapter [the council of Sisters who have the right to vote for the admission of a religious]. And in the probable case of her being accepted, of having her make profession in my hands, thus before the elections, which were to take place only later. But Mother Marie de Gonzague, who was hoping to be elected prioress in my place, wanted to postpone until after the elections the admission of my sister to religious profession. And she began a campaign among the chapter Sisters to have my sister sent to the Carmel of Saigon, which was asking for help.

Thérèse was thus going to be caught between the competency of her former and future prioress, Mother Marie de Gonzague, and her affection for her sister, Mother Agnès, who was the current prioress.

One gray day in January 1896, in the laundry, some fifteen of the Carmelites were doing the wash. Mother Marie de Gonzague was not there. A discussion arose on the subject of Céline's profession. Sister Aimée of Jesus, another witness at the canonization process, recounted: "Only once did I see my Sister Thérèse of the Child Jesus lose a little of her calm. Her sister Céline [in Carmel, Sister Geneviève] had been humiliated, and I said, speaking to no one in particular: 'Mother Marie de Gonzague, Mother Mistress, has a right to test this novice [Céline] like any other, so why be surprised?'"

It was then that a firm voice arose from the group and said: "There are some forms of testing that should not be used." Very moved, it was Thérèse who had spoken. It was the only time Thérèse expressed herself on the subject. And it was no small matter to imagine the departure of Céline, the sister she most loved, for Saigon. The following proved this.

Several days later, Sister Geneviève was presented to the chapter. The rule of Carmel provided that, where several sisters were present in the same monastery, the chapter Sisters would not vote for their own sister. That did not mean that she was not present in the chapter. Now an extraordinary thing took place at that time. Mother Marie de Gonzague, novice mistress, thus presented Sister Geneviève to the chapter for the decisive vote, but, during the vote, she left the mother prioress outside, behind the door. According to custom, after the vote, they had all the Sisters come in. Mother Marie de Gonzague left the prioress (that is, Mother Agnès, Thérèse's sister) standing there with the novices who had entered at the sound of the bell. Thus the three Martin sisters entered the chapter room only to hear the results of the vote: "Sister Geneviève is admitted." This episode earned us, moreover, one of the most beautiful texts ever written on heaven and the manner in which we will be received there. It is letter 182 from Thérèse to her sister, a superb letter of several pages.

*

That, then, was the only time Thérèse gave evidence of an emotional reaction to her prioress, although she must have had so many occasions to let her temper show. Far from feeling any impulse to be quick-tempered, Thérèse explicitly recognized the correctness of the discernment of Mother Marie de Gonzague, who had understood that it was necessary to treat her normally and not to be trapped by the group of Martin sisters. She even described Mother Marie de Gonzague's attitude as an "inestimable grace"! Five in the midst of a group of twenty-two: that could have been quite explosive. "She loved me very much", said Thérèse, in speaking of Mother Marie de Gonzague. "Nevertheless God permitted that she was VERY SEVERE *without her even being aware of it*. . . . What would have become of me if I had been the 'pet' of the community. . . ? Happily I was preserved from this misfortune. I *loved* Mother Prioress *very much*, but it was a pure affection which raised me to the Bridegroom of my soul" (SS 150–51).

3. *Sickness and Confinement of Her Father*

Ten days after Thérèse's clothing, which had been like a great feast day and a day of "triumph" for her father, a tragic event occurred. M. Martin experienced a time of depression. He bought a revolver in order to protect his daughters. The doctor decided to hospitalize him. Then, a month after Thérèse of Lisieux's clothing, her father was taken forcibly to the hospital of Bon-Sauveur, in Caen, which accommodated over two thousand sick people. Céline and Léonie were upset about it. Their uncle confided to one of his particularly close friends the care they took to make M. Martin believe they were going to take a walk, and that was the confinement. M. Martin would remain there more than three years. He was released when he became paralyzed. In four years, Thérèse would have but a single parlor visit with her father. She would see him again only once between his admission to the hospital and his death, which would take place several months after that last parlor visit, when, in his wheelchair, he could no longer speak, only make a gesture: "To heaven!" That was all.

That had been heartrending for Thérèse, especially because everyone talked about it in Lisieux. There was gossip, and Thérèse would say nothing. People insinuated that the father's illness was perhaps due to the fact that his daughters had entered the Carmel. Thérèse was nineteen years old when her father left the hospital.

Permit me to mention here the visual shortcut that film maker Alain Cavalier used in his film *Thérèse*. Very strict about historical correctness, deeply esteemed by all the best experts on Thérèse of Lisieux, Cavalier depicted the hardness of this last parlor visit for Thérèse by superimposing several anecdotes. A tear having run down M. Martin's face, someone dries it with a little handkerchief. Thérèse asks her prioress for permission to keep it. The latter simply remarks that she already has a family souvenir: the pen tray in her writing box. Thérèse consents. She will not even have one of her father's tears to keep. The cinematic license transcribes well Thérèse's deep emotion.

THREE FAMILY BLESSINGS IN CARMEL

1. *Thérèse Is the Last of the Martin Sisters*

Being the youngest child means a priori that one has no other weapon but that last place. That was indeed what she would have when, for example, she had to wait to read a letter from one of her sisters. She wrote coolly on July 12, 1896: "I would have answered your charming letter last Sunday if it had been given to me. But we are five, and you know I am the littlest . . . so I run the risk of not seeing the letters until after the others or else not at all . . . I saw your letter only on Friday" (LT 191, GC 2:965). This was clearly the situation, and we can imagine what it meant for Thérèse when it was a question of news of her father at the hospital.

Thérèse said how tempting it would have been to take advantage of this status as youngest child in order to seek consolation, for example, by chatting during the preparation of the refectory; she had at the time the same office as her sister Mother Agnès, and it would have been natural to use the occasion to exchange a few words, especially since this was when M. Martin had just been hospitalized. Thérèse wrote only: "There was the Rule to observe. I was unable to confide in you; after all, I was in Carmel and no longer at Les Buissonnets under the paternal roof!" (SS 160).

The writing of *Histoire d'une Âme* is significant. Mother Agnès was prioress. This was at the beginning of the year 1895. At recreation, Thérèse's oldest sister, Marie, was surprised by the memory of her young sister. She suggested to Mother Agnès, then prioress, that she ask Thérèse to recount her memories. Thérèse took a little looseleaf notebook. She began at the top of the first page and would stop quite simply at the bottom of the last. Mother Agnès recounted:

> One winter evening at the beginning of 1895, two and a half years before Sister Thérèse's death, when I was with my two sisters (Marie and Thérèse), Sister Thérèse of the Child Jesus was telling me a few things about her childhood, and Sister Marie of the Sacred Heart (my older sister Marie) said to me, "Oh, Mother, what a shame we don't have all that in writing! If you asked Sister Thérèse of the Child Jesus to write down her childhood memories for us, how entertaining that would be for us!" "I couldn't ask for anything better", I replied. Then, turning to Sister Thérèse of the Child Jesus, who was laughing as if we were making fun of her, I said: "I order you to write down all your childhood memories." The Servant of God set to work on it through obedience, for I was her prioress at the time. She wrote only during her free time and gave me her notebook on January 20, 1896, for my feast day. I was at evening prayer. When she passed by to go to her bench, Sister Thérèse of the Child Jesus knelt down and presented me with this treasure. I acknowledged it merely with a nod and put the manuscript on my bench without opening it. I did not take the time to read it until after the

elections in the spring of that same year. I noticed the Servant of God's virtue, for after her act of obedience, she thought no more of it at all and never asked me if I had read her notebook or what I thought of it. One day I told her that I had not had time to read any of it; she did not seem the slightest bit upset. (Mother Agnès, PO 146)

So Thérèse wrote. She did her duty and did not seek to know the effect produced or the profit she might draw from it. She obeyed since she was the youngest child, and here she was offering the world one of the most-translated books in the French language. At the time, her sister did not even read it. She would become truly aware of the value of that little notebook only shortly before Thérèse fell ill. Then Mother Agnès would regard her little Sister Thérèse differently and would realize that the "little one" had something exceptional to say. It was as if an express train passed in front of her, and she had to catch it en route. This would be why Mother Agnès and Sister Geneviève redoubled their care in gathering together the words Thérèse said during the last six months of her illness and death agony. Before this, Thérèse had always been the youngest child, the one who made spelling errors— which Mother Agnès corrected.

2. *A Happy Emulation*

Instead of being a pressure group, Thérèse's little family circle in Carmel became a laboratory of charity. A certain happy emulation could be discerned in it. Once again, this might have been ambivalent; it might have veered off, turned into a more or less studied affectivity, cultivated in isolation, indeed, exaggerated. This was not the case. The fact that they were a group obliged the best of them. This was a second blessing of having a family presence in the

Carmel. A happy, communicative joy was felt between the sisters and an authentic search for the best. The example of charity cited here, one among many others, shows once again how evident Thérèse's strength was on the occasion of an episode that was totally banal but which, to the attentive observer, gives a hint of the infinite secret it implied.

One day when the Carmelites were at recreation, with their sewing, just before Christmas, Thérèse realized that her neighbor was a little tense, excited. Now Thérèse, who was tall and strong, was asked to come to the door leading out to the street in order to help the gardener bring in the Christmas tree. Very few laypeople come inside a convent, a monastery: perhaps the plumber, the doctor. Rarely the gardener. Thérèse had a flash of inspiration. She knew her neighbor was dying of envy to go. For a Carmelite to have contact with someone from the outside was not, in fact, annoying. Thérèse then slowly folded up her work, in such a way that her neighbor got up, put away her own things more quickly, and said while rising: "Ah, Sister Thérèse, we can see you aren't in very much of a hurry to be of service." Sister Thérèse said nothing.

What would we have done? With a little bit of virtue, we would have said to our neighbor: "Oh, Sister, that would do you some good; it would relax you; you go in my place." We would already have made the fine gesture of giving up our place. With still a little more virtue, we would have discovered the stratagem of putting away our work slowly; but finding ourselves snubbed in front of the whole community, we would have said: "What? I find a way to let you go in my place, and this is all you have to say to me?" Thérèse not only said nothing, but added in thought: "Since that day, I have never again dared to judge anyone" (cf. SS 221–22; LC April 6, 1897, no. 3, pp. 36–37).

3. *The Initial Incomprehension of the Sisters*

What we have here is a happy paradox. It was manifested in, among other things, the initial attitude of Mother Agnès when, as prioress, she asked Thérèse to note down her memories. Mother Agnès did not suspect that this manuscript, which would become the beginning of the *Story of a Soul*, would have such importance. Whatever could or might be said about the faults of her sisters and of their "management" of Thérèse's case, it must be recognized that it was to the intuition of her sister Marie and to the request of her second sister, Mother Agnès, that we owe the *Story of a Soul*. Similarly, it must be recognized that we owe the second part of it, that called Manuscript B, which comprises pages worthy of Pascal, to the initial incomprehension of her oldest sister. One day when Thérèse explained to her that it was not a matter of having "great desires", Marie was troubled and thought that if she did not have great desires it was because she was not on the path of holiness. Thérèse then went on to explain to her her little way. It was not first of all desires, or the impression of having desires, that counted but confidence. It is the letter to Marie (LT 196) that forms the second part of the *Story of a Soul*, a text as important as the extraordinary passages from "My Vocation Is Love", the Act of Oblation, or the poem "Living on Love".

Finally we owe the *Last Conversations* in part to chance, which we could certainly call providential. When there proved to be scarcely any more hope for Thérèse's cure, since the Sister in charge of the infirmary was busy with the care of another sick Carmelite, Sister Hermance of the Heart of Jesus, the prioress, Mother Marie de Gonzague, confided Thérèse to her two sisters (cf. the information, wonderful in its detail, given by Guy Gaucher in his introduction to DE

32–48). So, Mother Agnès and Sister Geneviève, having finally discovered the charism of the youngest child, went on
to note down her reflections, day by day. It is possible to
reconstruct the diary of Thérèse's six last months, with all the
exchanges and conversations she had during that time, her
state of health, the visits and care she received (cf. ibid., 147–
86). A comprehensive comparison of these last conversations
set down in writing by the different witnesses is striking. It is
not a matter simply of a few leaves put together after the fact
through a misplaced affection, but rather the rereading of an
entire life in the face of death and of Christ. It is as if Thérèse
had, with the help of her sisters and particularly of Mother
Agnès, relived the graces of her life by following a divine,
theological, and terribly realistic psychoanalysis, since it was
the question of an "anamnesis", as the psychologists say, of
someone who knew she was going to die. Now, it is to her
sisters that we owe the memory, trace, and details of what
became the *Novissima Verba* and then the *Last Conversations*.
Mother Agnès and Sister Geneviève collected and noted
down, day by day, sometimes on simple journal leaves—some
of these have been preserved in the archives of Lisieux—all
the phrases, prayers, remarks, and reflections of their sister.
When Thérèse fell gravely ill, Mother Agnès had just read the
first part of her sister's reminiscences. She pursued Thérèse,
during her final months, with questions, requests for details,
as if she had a presentiment of what was at stake in her sister's
thoughts. Thérèse gave her, moreover, the mission to publish.
She was explicitly aware of the importance of her message. It
was again at the suggestion of Mother Agnès that Mother
Marie de Gonzague asked Thérèse to complete the account
of her life. That would be Manuscript C, in which Thérèse
was careful to return to two points she thought she had not
discussed sufficiently in the first part: prayer and charity.

*

Psychological Inevitabilities and False Gifts

If Thérèse owed in large part to her father her understanding
of the paternity of God, of the inner mystery of the Christian
God, if she owed in large part to her sisters and to her
Carmelite family her understanding of the communion of
saints, of the mystery of the Church, and of the love to be re-
created in a group, may we dare to ask: Did Thérèse, in larger
part than one might think and in a rather hidden way, owe to
her mother and to everything involved in the privation of
her presence the discovery of her little way and of the light
that it proposed? What we have here is indeed the strength
that made her a Doctor of the Church. We have indeed a
"message". She herself named it this by implying that it would
be necessary to make it known. She was aware of being its
bearer.

One could of course bring up the fact that Thérèse made
no explicit mention at all of her mother during the last
months of her life. The psychoanalysis used by Jacques
Maître, in the book *L'Orpheline de la Bérésina, Thérèse de
Lisieux. Essai de psychanalyse socio-historique* (Paris, 1995),
which we would describe as "labored", retraces at length
Thérèse's infantile regressions. Is this enough in order to enter into the mystery or even the reality? If I may be permitted
a personal remark. Like Thérèse, the author was part of a
family of nine children. Like Thérèse, he lost his mother very
early, when he was younger than Thérèse, no more than
eighteen months old. Now these facts have greatly helped the
author sense, from within, many of Thérèse's intuitions. I
have counted carefully. I do not remember having explicitly
talked about my mother—memories, allusions, evocations—

more than six or seven times in my life. Would that mean that her presence did not play a very great part in my existence? I had to wait until I was fifty-eight years old to discover, by chance, a photograph album and to find there something other than the memory of her likeness that I kept of her at the time she was exhausted by illness. I saw the joie de vivre of a young woman, of a young girl, of a little girl who was my mother, of a face younger than my own. My father spoke to me at length of her once, with tenderness, details, nearly confidences. I was thirty-seven years old. Does the rarity of such talks mean that my mother was not very consciously present in my thoughts, my prayer, or my decisions? Certainly not. How many times have I peacefully, simply known that she played a decisive role. I have never experienced the need to talk about it. She was present when, as children, we concluded evening prayer with this invocation; "Suzanne, pray for us." Why would this experience, about which I have often thought in getting to know the life of Thérèse of Lisieux since 1944, not help me in examining it anew? Did Thérèse's mother and all the memories she kept of her not play a greater role than has been thought—and a simpler one than the methods and fantasies to which the psychoanalysts strive to reduce it?

Why, then, not dare to suggest that we owe Thérèse's message also to her family? To turn aggressiveness into hope and trust, despite all the hardships of existence such as Thérèse experienced, which would have been enough to crush or discourage anyone else; to break through the psychological inevitabilities that were being formulated, in an abstract, areligious, and somewhat tragic way, by Freud and psychoanalysis at that very time; to rediscover, three-quarters of a century before the Council, both the sense of the transcendent mercy of God and the infinite value of the Incarnation

and of all the details of our life, all in language that was concrete, accessible, and theologically impeccable—that was the
genius of Thérèse, and why not be grateful to her family for
having helped her? Certainly, there are traumatizing elements
in every life, bereavements, misfortunes, lack of understanding, mazes, inexplicable delays. Thérèse shows that even that
which crushes can, through grace, serve the good. Would this
be insignificant at a time when mankind, clutching its psychology with all the scientific greed with which it is at times
capable of investing it, has some difficulty in keeping a certain
magnetic north with gentleness of heart? That would merit
the consideration of a "doctorate".

To sum up: Misfortunes give birth in human existence to two
things: dissatisfaction and aggressiveness. Who would dare say
that a family is not a false gift? A mother is never done with
her children, even at the twilight of her life. No one is ever
done with his companions: former professors, officials, asso-
ciates, or others. Who has finished with his in-laws? Who
with his community, his parish, his group? Thérèse would
have had every reason to be dissatisfied, aggressive, or bitter.
Certainly she had happy moments. One could say, at best,
two years: 1886, the year of her conversion, and 1895, the
year of her Act of Oblation. Now, in the face of all that she
did not choose in her life, she never raised her voice; she
never sought to establish a relationship of force. Thérèse's
greatest virtue was not first of all the tenacious will to accomplish some work, to attain some goal, no matter how great, to
accede to the first place, to participate in the world championship of holiness. It was not the appetite for victory. The
ultimate adventure proposed to Thérèse was the love of a
Person, the will no longer to act except for another and for
what constitutes love: trust, or, more exactly, abandonment

to this other, and at the very moment when everything could have led to flight, aggressiveness, or despair. Thérèse no longer pursued a goal or a work. She loved, and for that she relied on this assurance: Someone watched over her; someone went before her; someone responded to her. Apparently *everything* had failed. Only one certitude still remained: that of total trust in another. We can never sufficiently stress the kindness of God, who permitted Thérèse to benefit from the family conditions that were hers.

CHAPTER FIVE

The Greatness of the Everyday

All Is Given, All Remains to Be Done

Thérèse had acquired the habit of smiling every time when, at work, she was disturbed by a Sister who came, with or without reason, to ask her for some service. She noted this with humor in her last manuscript. She was ready for annoyance: "I want it; I count on it . . . so, I am always happy" (CSG 104).

We are now in mid-June 1897. For eight days she had been certain that her illness was incurable. At the end of her strength, she sometimes took more than half an hour to climb the stairs of a terrace that adjoined her cell. She braced herself, exhausted from fever, in order to write the rest of her reminiscences as obedience required. Installed in the garden in the wheelchair that her paralyzed father had used, she recounted: "Recently, I was writing on charity and, very often, the nuns came to distract me; then I was very careful not to become impatient, to put into practice what I was writing about" (LC June 15, no. 5, p. 66).

> When I begin to take up my pen, behold a Sister who passes by, a pitchfork on her shoulder. She believes she will distract me with a little idle chatter: hay, ducks, hens, visits

of the doctor, everything is discussed; to tell the truth, this doesn't last a long time, but there is *more than one good charitable Sister*, and all of a sudden another hay worker throws flowers on my lap, perhaps believing these will inspire me with poetic thoughts. I am not looking for them at the moment and would prefer to see the flowers remain swaying on their stems. Finally, fatigued by opening and shutting this famous copybook, I open a book (which doesn't want to stay open) and say resolutely that I shall copy out some thoughts from the psalms and the Gospels for the feast of Our Mother. It's very true that I am not sparing in these quotes.

Dear Mother, I would amuse you, I believe, when telling you about all my adventures in the groves of Carmel; I don't know if I have been able to write ten lines without being disturbed; this should not make me laugh nor amuse me; however, for the love of God and my Sisters (so charitable towards me) I take care to appear happy and especially *to be so*. For example, here is a hay worker who is just leaving me after having said very compassionately: "Poor little Sister, it must tire you out writing like that all day long." "Don't worry," I answer, "I appear to be writing very much, but really I am writing almost nothing." "Very good!" she says, "but just the same, I am very happy we are doing the haying since this always distracts you a little." In fact, it is such a great distraction for me. (SS 227–28)

Very sensitive herself, she knew from personal experience the upset caused by tactlessness or ungracious remarks. At the time of her father's mental illness, those were not in short supply. Thérèse willed to see, beyond these terrible spikes, or "pinpricks", as she called them, only "the gentle hand of [her] Jesus" (LT 55, GC 1:442). And she knew that the least of her sufferings, offered with love, could save a soul.

What to Do with Antipathy?

Thérèse saw very quickly in community that antipathies were often caused by letting oneself be obsessed by the most conspicuous faults of those around one instead of detecting their good points.

> There is in the Community a Sister who has the faculty of displeasing me in everything, in her ways, her words, her character, everything seems *very disagreeable* to me. And still, she is a holy religious who must be very pleasing to God. Not wishing to give in to the natural antipathy I was experiencing, I told myself that charity must not consist in feelings but in works; then I set myself to doing for this Sister what I would do for the person I loved the most. Every time I met her I prayed to God for her, offering Him all her virtues and merits. I felt this was pleasing to Jesus. (SS 222)

There we have Thérèse faced with antipathy. Her reaction was immediately positive; she was not content with resisting aversion toward a Sister whose somewhat "stilted" character annoyed her profoundly; she told herself that there had to be qualities and merit in her that God alone knew. Let us go on reading:

> I wasn't content simply with praying very much for the Sister who gave me so many struggles, but I took care to render her all the services possible, and when I was tempted to answer her back in a disagreeable manner, I was content with giving her my most friendly smile, and with changing the subject. . . .
>
> Frequently, when I . . . had occasion to work with this Sister, I used to run away like a deserter whenever my struggles became too violent. As she was absolutely unaware of my feelings for her, never did she suspect the motives for my conduct, and she remained convinced that her character

was very pleasing to me. One day at recreation she asked in almost these words: "Would you tell me, Sister Thérèse of the Child Jesus, what attracts you so much towards me; everytime you look at me, I see you smile?" Ah!, what attracted me was Jesus hidden in the depths of her soul. (SS 222–23)

What Thérèse wrote in the *Story of a Soul* must be completed by the confession of her older sister Marie, during the canonization process:

She hid [her dislike] so well that, thinking she loved this Sister very much, I felt somewhat jealous, and I said to her one day: "I cannot help confiding to you something that's grieving me. . . . I think you love Sister [Thérèse of Saint Augustine] more than me; and I don't think that's fair, for, after all, God made family ties. But you always seem so happy to see her that I can't think anything else, since you've never shown such pleasure about being with me." She laughed heartily at this, but she confided none of the feelings of aversion this religious caused her. (PO 250–52; read also DE 786–89, especially the top of 788)

Let us listen to this laughter and this silence. It was only through an indiscretion that the Sister, thirty years after the death of Thérèse, discovered that it was she who was the subject of the account in the *Story of a Soul*. Although all the religious in the Carmel had been very well aware of it, she had not recognized herself, still persuaded of having been a consolation for Saint Thérèse (cf. *Summarium*, p. 424; PA 1082). That the community had never betrayed it was much to its credit. Up to the day when Canon Travert, chaplain to the Carmel, exasperated by the aforesaid Sister, revealed to her in a flash of temper that she was the one in question.

*

In the final months of her life, she insistently returned to the second commandment of the gospel: "I understood it before, it is true, but . . . I had never fathomed the meaning of these words of Jesus: '*The second commandment is like the first.*'. . . It is no longer a question of loving one's neighbor as oneself but of loving him as *He, Jesus, has loved him*, and will love him to the consummation of the ages" (SS 219–20). Far from finding this impossible, Thérèse adds:

> Ah! Lord, I know you don't command the impossible. You know better than I do my weakness. . . . You know very well that never would I be able to love my Sisters as You love them, unless You, O my Jesus, loved them in me. . . . Oh! how I love this new commandment since it gives me the assurance that Your Will is to love in me all those You command me to love! (SS 221).

But Thérèse concludes: "It is love alone that counts" (DE, vol. 2, "Annexes", p. 482). "To love You as You love me, I would have to borrow Your own Love, and then only would I be at rest" (SS 256).

Nothing Diverts Me

In a simple, true way, Thérèse demonstrates the laws of the second conversion. Like Saint Peter after his betrayal, like Saint Paul, Saint Augustine, Saint Francis, and Joan of Arc. The second conversion is to follow Someone, to agree to sever all ties, to commit oneself to a path where it is no longer a question of choosing Christ and Christianity but of preferring them. The first conversion is often rough but is at times attractive; the second often appears impossible without objecting. Thérèse indicates the path in concrete terms: in everyday life, to do the truth, but in the name of a love that comes from above and that then transcends strictures, petty details, or a settling of scores.

Thérèse, in her most simple and direct life, believed that it was in the events of every day that God comes, a God who is present and who says to each of us: "Will you?" "Nothing diverts me", she says, "nothing destroys my plans. Nothing at all." It would be difficult to find a better advance commentary on the central constitution of Vatican II than the account of her life. "Accordingly all Christians, in the conditions, duties and circumstances of their life and through all these, will sanctify themselves more and more if they receive all things with faith from the hand of the heavenly Father and cooperate with the divine will, thus showing forth in that temporal service the love with which God has loved the world" (*Lumen Gentium*, no. 41).

> The event comes to me then literally as a present from God, present in the twofold sense of the word presence and of the word gift. This present moment comes to me wrapped in an action that is offered to or asked of me. To make one's bed or to celebrate Mass, to peel vegetables or to receive Communion, to wait for a bus or to pray, at every moment the action that is offered to me is the presence that God takes in my life.[1]

Cold Water and Artificial Flowers

One of her novices, undoubtedly the one Thérèse loved the most, surely the liveliest of her companions, a "Parisian" and mischievous, kept many memories.[2] Her testimony at the process was one of the most invaluable and the most vivid:

---

[1] J. Loew, *Comme s'il voyait l'invisible* (Paris, Cerf), 139–40.

[2] Cf. the very fine book by Pierre Descouvemont, *Soeur Marie de la Trinité, une novice de sainte Thérèse* (Paris: Cerf, 1985).

One day I asked her which was better, to go rinse in cold water, or stay in the laundry to wash with hot water. She replied, "Oh, that's not difficult to know! If you find it hard to go to the cold water, that means the rest find it hard, too; so, you go. But if, on the other hand, it's a hot day, you should prefer to stay in the laundry. By taking the worst places, you both mortify yourself and practice charity toward others, because you leave the best places for them." After that, I understood why I saw her in the laundry when it was hot, and precisely in the place that had the least air! I also witnessed acts of heroic charity she practiced with the religious of whom she speaks in her Life, the one who had the knack of being disagreeable in everything. She lavished such esteem and affection on her that one would have to have believed she had a particular affection for her. (PO 459)

We have already recalled above the very convincing story of the Christmas tree, an anecdote that is exemplary in its commonplaceness! Let us also point out another one that resembles it. One old mother was allergic to perfume (CSG 97). And then someone made a gift to the Carmel of some artificial flowers. Thérèse put them by the cloister statue. On leaving the chapel, she sensed the old Sister begin to get angry. What would we have done? The normal reflex would have been to take a little revenge by letting the Sister protest and make herself ridiculous in public. With a little kindness, we could emphasize that the fear was pointless, since the flowers were artificial. Thérèse did more; she took the initiative and said: "Oh, my Mother, look how well they imitate nature nowadays. . . ." Thérèse, with one word, had "drawn close", she had been a neighbor.

*

One of her biographers, in looking for her limitations—
certainly she had some—stressed that "Thérèse had no political dimension." Of course, she was not involved in politics,
but that does not mean that her life did not have any political
dimension. In fact, would it not be the greatest political
victory—I do indeed say political—for a Christian today to
learn this victory of charity, and particularly that which consists of refusing to classify, to divide men into "good" and
"bad", and thus to reject that mortal illness called Manicheism: to refuse to think that there might be a parallel good
and bad and thus a bad that would in the end escape love.
Thérèse's revolution was to prove the opposite, and to prove
that it is possible in life, in everyday life. There is no "bad to
be eliminated". For Thérèse, in the end love alone will triumph beyond all battles, classes, interests, or groups.

> Your child, however, O Lord, . . . begs pardon for her
> brothers. She is resigned to eat the bread of sorrow as long
> as You desire it; she does not wish to rise up from this table
> filled with bitterness at which poor sinners are eating until
> the day set by You. . . . May all those who were not enlight-
> ened by the bright flame of faith one day see it shine. O
> Jesus! if it is needful that the table soiled by them be purified
> by a soul who loves You, then I desire to eat this bread of
> trial at this table until it pleases You to bring me into Your
> bright Kingdom. (SS 212)

Thérèse with her sister Céline in 1881.

"Céline had become the intimate confidante of my thoughts."

Thérèse at thirteen years.

February 1886. Marie, Thérèse's older sister and godmother, had just entered Carmel. There were thus already two of her sisters in the convent, which led her to a relapse into poor health: "I no longer had anyone in whom to confide", she said.

Thérèse in Carmel.

Thérèse at sixteen. Because of the threat of expulsions, she still had all her hair, underneath her veil. Her hair was cut only later.

The four Martin sisters and the mother prioress.
First photo of the family, in June 1894.

© OFFICE CENTRAL DE LISIEUX

Céline, who had remained with her ill father, was able to enter Carmel
after his death. In a white mantle, seated at the left is the mother prioress,
whom one of Thérèse's novices nicknamed "the wolf". Thérèse was opposed
to any assault on her. She loved her mother prioress profoundly.

Shortly before the Act of Oblation to Merciful Love.

The happy year of the Act of Oblation: April 15, 1895.

At the wash. April 19, 1895.

Thérèse: the last pose.

© OFFICE CENTRAL DE LISIEUX

June 7, 1897. Two days later, Thérèse learned that there was no hope for recovery. She posed one last time, on her knees in the middle of the cloister, with the two symbols that dominated her life: the Infant Jesus and the Holy Face.

"We would like to suffer generously—what an illusion!"

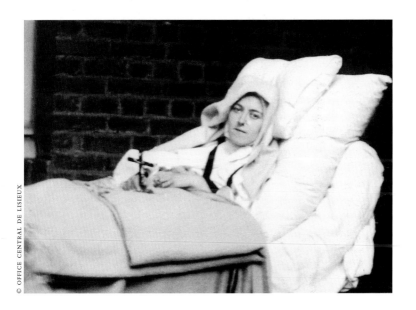

August 30, 1897. Thérèse had known since June 8 that she would not recover. From August 19 on, she was no longer able to receive even a fragment of the Host. On August 30, on her wheeled bed, she was moved under the cloister for a last visit to the Blessed Sacrament. She is picking the petals off roses on her crucifix. She died on September 30.

PART TWO

HER GOD

CHAPTER SIX

The "Secret"

"He was teaching me in secret about the things of his love." That is how Thérèse summed up the blessed time of happy conversations she carried on in the belvedere in the garden of Les Buissonnets with her sister and confidante Céline when the desire for Carmel was becoming more and more pressing within her. Thérèse would use this word "secret" fifty-seven times. "I know your secrets, for I am your spouse. / O my divine Savior / I fall asleep on your Heart. / It is mine!" she wrote in poem no. 24, "Jesus, My Beloved, Remember! . . ." (PST 128). She insists in another important poem ["Why I Love You, O Mary"]: "Doesn't its [the Gospel's] profound silence / Reveal that *The Eternal Word Himself* / *Wants to sing the secrets of your life*" (PN 54, PST 220). That obliges us to ask three questions, without which we would miss the essence of Thérèse of Lisieux.

What, then, is this secret?

How does Thérèse understand love? Can we rely solely on the experience of great women lovers in order to understand it? The descriptions given by Jean Chalon in his biography *Thérèse de Lisieux, une vie d'amour* [1] are interesting, but the references to Liane de Pougy, to Colette, and to George Sand

---

[1] Jean Chalon, *Thérèse de Lisieux, une vie d'amour* (Paris: Cerf, 1996).

cannot suffice to introduce us to what Thérèse lived (see appendix 2).

And finally, why is there not greater respect for what Thérèse says so well herself, that is, that the Person with whom she is speaking is not only Jesus but the Son and the Divine Word in the movement of trinitarian love that draws her toward his Father? The One with whom Thérèse converses, Jesus, is the sole being in the world whose very Person, being divine, exists only in a state of love relationship to his source. One could never say of Buddha or Muhammad or of any prophet, as sublime as he might be, what Thérèse says of Jesus. That changes everything. For Thérèse, the Trinity is not an abstract idea but the Life that orients, prioritizes, and organizes her whole existence. The decisive moments of her life are clear to all: her First Communion, her entrance into Carmel, her veiling, her Act of Oblation. That the word "Trinity" is not mentioned even once in a biography like that of Jean Chalon is at the very least surprising. The love that motivates Thérèse presupposes, not merely a difference in degree with respect to human loves, but a difference in nature. She clarifies this very well: "To love, I have to borrow Your own love."

Certainly it is astounding what an exceptional understanding and discernment of "the things of love" Thérèse had very early in her life. Knowing only of the very many lines on that subject, we might justifiably be shocked by the audacity, realism, and fervor with which Thérèse speaks of love. It is precisely because it is a question of a different nature of love that all the audacity is possible. And that is one more reason to investigate her secret—which is indeed the secret of all those who love—and for not being satisfied with mere descriptions, however glowing. For Thérèse leads us much farther. It is a question of a "secret". What is it?

A twofold wish carries all love toward its accomplishment. On the one hand, the wish not to be alone any more and, for that purpose, the wish that the other might be, first of all, truly, a partner. But, paradoxically, if love wishes to make the other as free, as "firm", as responsible as possible, it is in order to satisfy a second wish, which, chronologically, may be prior: the wish to let oneself be drawn by the other so as henceforth to be but one with him.

If we need the other to exist, it is indeed in order that he might be yet more capable of amazing and attracting us, arousing in us the attention, magnetization, and the blessed "wound" that makes it impossible to do without him. There is an involution, a circular movement, a reciprocal causality between these two impulses. Both at the beginning and at the end, respect for the other is imperative for the one who loves as the indispensable condition so that we might pour ourselves into him and be henceforth but one with him. On the one hand, we want to venerate him, admire him, discover his wealth of qualities, but in order to be better able to offer ourselves to him. The one who loves needs to pay homage out of his own poverty to the one whose fulfilling attraction he has felt.

What kind of affection would it be if the other were only something vague, reduced to being only an impression or an idea, an idol, an object fabricated or fantasized, one means among others? What would a religion be that reduced God or the Transcendent to being only "the condition of self-realization" (Drewermann)?

An initial weakening has acted as seduction, attraction, "wound". Whatever the terms used, any philosophy, any psychology, even analytical, any mysticism must recognize that the phenomena of love are never transcribed in a satisfactory way in theoretical, abstract, notional terms. Love puts goodness and the final cause into play. Now what belongs to the good is the sole order of things that requires two ends to exist: both a lovable reality and the recognition of this reality as adapted and conformed to the fullness of the one who loves. There is no love until this conformity is perceived— and not abstractly, but concretely—as drawing toward the "most" that completes and brings to rest the one who has recognized his lack. In order that the initial weakening might be pursued and not remain merely a part of the realm of animal impulse, of search for a prey, of the sole concern to appease the need for satisfaction, love discovers the primary attitude necessary to endure. It is Thérèse's "before God". The more she sees how great the Other is, the more she is filled. The more the Other exists, the more she desires that he remain in his transcendence. Then the more she can please him despite—and because of—her littleness, to the point of discovering very quickly that she would like to take his place. Since he exists, an exchange of hearts can be achieved. It is no longer a question of proving to ourselves that we are strong, capable, autonomous; it is no longer a question of increasing our value, since we no longer want to act only for ourselves but, first of all, for the Other, in order to "please him", to "answer his expectations", as Thérèse says. We pass from the mere search for a prey to respect for his boundaries, respect that alone proves that we have crossed the threshold of a human, spiritual, and not merely bestial love.

In this way, the second wish of love can succeed without prejudice: the need for union, to be henceforth but one with the person we love. Aspiring toward union becomes no longer dangerous or debilitating since it ensues from the respect for reciprocity. We become increasingly happy with what the Other demands. The alliance can take place when each brings what he is: God, everything; Thérèse, nothing, and, what is more: a deformed nothing that is not only poor and fragile but at times sinful and rebellious.

That God is Father, that God loves what he makes, and that he carries on his creation tirelessly: many religions sense this. Following the Gospels, Saint John, Isaiah, and all the mystics, Thérèse lived and teaches much more.

How could we sum up the Bible if not by a dialogue between God and humanity? The Creator, contrary to anything one might expect, comes patiently, endlessly, tirelessly to say and repeat to humanity: "You are what counts." And humanity does not understand, up to the day when Christ allows himself to be crucified in order to show how far the Creator will go in his desire to make us understand why he has created us. It was not for nothing that Thérèse was very sensitive to the reading of the prophet Isaiah. We find there this formidable announcement: "Your builder will marry you." And God is waiting for us to respond to him in turn: "No, Lord, you are what counts." And God will echo our reply. An extraordinary dialogue, which is that of the saints and mystics. In the mystery of the Cross, Thérèse discovered that God became a beggar for love in the agony just as at Christmas. She constantly returned to this discovery of the mendicant Christ.

What Is Love?

At the end of the first movement of love, one word sums up everything: reciprocity. Here, we are at the heart of the secret of love in its perfect state. The concern for reciprocity includes both respect and intensity. It was the genius of the theology of Saint Thomas Aquinas to dare to say that this reciprocity expressed the essence of Christian charity and revealed the newness of it. For his masters and predecessors, including Peter Lombard, charity could not be anything "created". One could not say that man was invited to enter fully as a partner of divine love and go as far as what Saint John of the Cross would call "giving God to God". What was blasphemy for Jewish thought at the time of Christ, what is defilement for Islam, and is still incomprehensible, for example, for the great Protestant exegete Nygren in his thesis *Agape and Eros*, Thérèse of Lisieux grasped very well: Charity is of a different nature from love and is not merely a matter of a difference of degree with respect to human affectivity in its limits.

It is the recourse to "friendship", in a rigorous fidelity to the Gospels, that allows theology to justify fully the reality of charity, lived by Christians and expressed by saints and mystics. Insofar as charity was likened solely to the presence of the Holy Spirit, it could not really be attributed to man. It was the presence of a Divine Person, but it could not slip into the feelings of a limited creature. Thanks to his understanding of the order proper to love and to divine causality, Thomas Aquinas freed the whole history of thinking about the relationship between man and God. When he dared to define charity by friendship and then friendship by reciprocity in the exchange of love itself, he accounted for evangelical revelation, fully justified the expression of the mystics, manifested the newness—scandalous for some—of Christianity, and also, dare we say, helped to put in their place the at times laborious groping of modern psychologies and psychoanalysis on this point.

To understand Thérèse's expressions in their marvelous audacity and accuracy, let us clarify briefly the intuition of theology. Charity is a friendship. What does that mean? First of all, a love in the perfect state. That presupposes three things:

—A love that wants good for another, a benevolent, not possessive, love, not a love that monopolizes but one that wants the good of the other. Now that does not suffice to define friendship. There must be two more characteristics;

—Friendship speaks of a love that is mutual, responding to each other. And that, too, does not suffice;

—It is also necessary that this reciprocity be founded on an exchange, but not on just any exchange whatever. A sympathy can be founded on the most varied exchanges. A friendship can be born from multiple points of convergence: they both like music, sports, sharing ideas, travels, religion, devotion to or a struggle for some specific cause. This is not love in its perfect state. There is truly friendship and love in the perfect state only when the object of the exchange is love itself.

One of the times when a priest trembles most in his life is during the marriage preparation of future spouses; will they know how to respect each other to the point of wanting to be the source of autonomy, to the point of respecting each other not only for their good qualities or for the benefits that one can draw from the other, but as persons, irreducible in themselves, and infinite because they are the divine image of God? There is complete love only if one loves the other because the other loves him to the point of becoming the source of his being, of his happiness. The nourishment of love-friendship in its complete state is to know and to repeat to oneself ceaselessly that what arouses the other is the joy he expects from our love.

It was indeed this mystery that Thérèse understood very early and maintained throughout her life. In 1890, she wrote to Céline: "You know that I myself do not see the Sacred Heart as everybody else. I think that the Heart of my Spouse is mine alone, just as mine is His alone, and I speak to Him then in the solitude of this delightful heart to heart, while waiting to contemplate Him one day face to face" (LT 122, October 14, 1890, GC 2:709). And on July 13, 1897, on her deathbed, she would say with still more audacity to her sister Mother Agnès: "God will have to carry out my will in heaven because I have never done my own will here on earth" (LC July 13, no. 2, p. 91).

A Happy Madness

Thérèse discovered that the intimate reciprocity of true love presupposes a certain death to oneself, a disarmament, a self-effacement that is madness, but a happy madness. For some, it is true, that seems sentimental. For others, it would perhaps be reserved for a few privileged cases. For still others, it would make life worth living. For others, finally, it is what God himself sought to establish with mankind and what alone deserves to be the reason for living. In the rosary, why do we say the Our Father once and the Hail Mary ten times? Because it is relatively easy to say to someone: "I love you"; that is the Our Father, and we can believe that that is true. But to believe that we are loved, we must hear it said ten times. Christ, after the Resurrection, did not ask Peter, who had betrayed him, "Are you sorry? Are you ready to leave your anguish behind? Have you seen how weak you are?" He only asked: "Peter, do you love me? Peter, do you love me more than these others?"

It is in the name of this reciprocity that Christ wants us to exist. It was on this that Thérèse focused. She knew that God expected her trust, that she could please him, that she could respond to his wish; she knew that, because he loved her, he wished her autonomy. Then, like the Good Samaritan, she could quench his thirst at the edge of the well; she could be "before him" like the cedar of Lebanon, like the palm tree of which the psalms speak, and merit, act, offer. It is in this respect that she would be different from Luther. Thérèse knew that the least act has a sacred value in the eyes of God because it becomes a response of love; she had the audacity to think of herself as princess and queen for her king; she could have control over him because it was he who wished it. Let us read once again the unimaginable text of her wedding announcement, written as an invitation to her veiling ceremony. She entitled it: "Letter of Invitation to the Wedding of Sister Thérèse of the Child Jesus of the Holy Face". These lines follow:

Almighty God, Creator of Heaven and earth, Sovereign Ruler of the World, and the Most Glorious Virgin Mary, Queen and Princess of the heavenly Court, wish to invite you to the wedding of their Divine Son Jesus, King of Kings and Lord of Lords, to Mademoiselle Thérèse Martin, now Lady and Princess of the kingdoms brought as dowry by her Divine Spouse, namely, the Childhood of Jesus and His Passion, her titles of nobility being: of the Child Jesus and of the Holy Face.

Monsieur Louis Martin, Proprietor and Owner of the Domains of Suffering and Humiliation, and Madame Martin, Princess and Lady of honor of the Heavenly Court, wish to invite you to the wedding of their Daughter Thérèse to Jesus, the Word of God, Second Person of the Adorable Trinity, who, through the Operation of the Holy Spirit, was made Man and Son of Mary, the Queen of Heaven.

And Thérèse adds:

Unable to invite you to the nuptial blessing given on the mountain of Carmel [September 8, 1890] (the heavenly Court alone was admitted), they beg you, nonetheless, to be present at the return from the Wedding which will take place tomorrow, on the Day of Eternity, to which Day Jesus, the

Son of God, will come on the clouds of Heaven to judge the
Living and the Dead.

The hour is uncertain as yet, so you are invited to hold
yourselves in readiness and to watch. (L 118, GC 1:679-80)

Three "Interesting" Realities in Existence

This invitation to Thérèse's commitment in religious life, in
the image of a wedding invitation, shows by its explicitly
trinitarian reference that Thérèse understood that three realities were interesting in existence: human love, mystical love,
and the Trinity. One can live alone and still live intensely
with genius, poetry, action, generosity, but one dies of it.
Love taught Thérèse that one lives intensely only if love/
friendship arouses that feeling of dissolving, disintegration,
and when, in appearance or in reality, one is completely given
to another being, one would dare to say "experienced" in
another, accepted by him. She knows by heart, in her prayer,
the passages from Saint John: ". . . even as thou, Father, art in
me, and I in thee. . . . The glory which thou hast given me I
have given to them, that they may be one even as we are one,
I in them and thou in me. . . . I made known to them thy
name, . . . that the love with which thou hast loved me may
be in them, and I in them" (Jn 17:21–26).

In true human love, those who love each other feel that they
are but one. They have this feeling of disintegration. And yet,
in this paradox of love, they remain two, for love respects the
distinction of each. A love is ravenous but, at the same time,
infinitely respectful and delicate. The other is at once necessary and implacable. "I can't live without you", but "You
escape me by becoming necessary." True love does not de-
vour. It respects the one who is loved. It is the one who loves

who lets himself be devoured by love. He lets himself dissolve
in the other. He who loves is the one who is possessed by the
other and not the one who possesses. We are one because
love unites us; we are two because love respects us. We are
three because love transcends us. It is the trinitarian mystery
itself: the Divine Persons are One because Love unites them;
they are Two in the infinite distinction of their "procession".
They "proceed", one from the other; they are distinguished
from each other, not in some rough, vague way, but infinitely
more than we are able to do. It is the divine, irreducible
property of trinitarian Love. In God, the intimacy is born
with which one engenders the other and with which, in
common, they express their mutual love. Thus the Divine
Persons are Three, in that reciprocal Love that is a Person: the
Holy Spirit. The entire life and thought of Thérèse of Lisieux
rested on this jubilant admiration of the trinitarian life. As we
recalled, when one loves, there is indeed in oneself a presence
of what one loves, and it is totally different from the presence
of an idea or fantasy; this presence is experienced as harmony,
accommodation, suitability, a mutual adaptation to fullness
and thus also as wound, thirst, expectation, response to a lack,
seduction, attraction of this fullness that leaves no repose until
the other is totally given. Thérèse understood that the Holy
Spirit is this common attraction, that the Father and the Son
test for what they have in common: that fullness of life that is
the divine nature they share with each other. In the human
being, this attraction is close to an imperfection; the other is
exterior to him. God possesses himself perfectly. In his Word,
he contemplates himself fully, as another self. He is love in the
measure of the repose that he takes in his own goodness.
Thérèse feels invited by the presence of the Holy Spirit to
that impulse of love that the Father and Son have in common
from the fact that they have the same existence, that they

share everything together. Thérèse abandons herself to that joy of Christ when he knew how the Father had entrusted everything to him and when that was the source in him of a secret adoration. "Those whom the Father has entrusted to me, that is what is most precious to me."

The Three Divine Activities

The mystery of the Holy Trinity often seems to Christians to be a bit abstract, distant, even secondary although unavoidable. Thérèse of Lisieux and, following her, Blessed Elizabeth of the Trinity, a Carmelite in Dijon who would die at the beginning of the twentieth century at about the same age as Thérèse, having been very inspired by the latter, are providential messengers sent to remind Christians that there is no more concrete, near-to-hand, or nourishing a mystery than that of the inner life of God. Of course one can, and even theologians (such as Edward Schillebeeckx) never hesitate to, consider reflections on the relations of the three Persons of the Holy Trinity to be "cold" or to "convey nothing". One can also understand, as did Saint John and Saint Paul and, following them, all the saints and councils, that the mystery of trinitarian love is the cornerstone of all that is new in the Christian reality. The four great treatises on the Trinity in the West, those of Saint Augustine, Saint Hilary, Richard of Saint-Victor, and Saint Thomas Aquinas, are wonderful. It is easy to find in them only an aesthetic satisfaction. That is not enough. The Trinity is not the product of fine arts or of a more or less rare experience reserved for a few. Every baptized person is invited to know that he is loved and invited to the table of God. Thérèse of Lisieux perceived that the source of her prayer, of her virtuous life, of the animation of her contemplative and apostolic life was trinitarian.

That deserves a brief and easy explanation. It is true that if everything is simple in God, the poverty of our concepts, ideas, and analyses obliges us to discern in him three types of activity:

1. Creation. It is common to all three Persons. Its result is an effect that is "external" to God, the product of the three Persons in their unity;

2. The inner secret of the Three. This is what, following the Gospels, is called the divine "processions". The Son is engendered by the Father. He says to the Father all that he is. And the Father and the Son give each other mutually the love by which they are loved, which is the Holy Spirit. This is the unfathomable Absolute that refers to nothing and to which nothing is referred. It is the "circumincession", the exchange, the blessed circulation of divine life between the Three. The Spirit is the link, the communion that "breathes out" and expresses the love of the Father and of the Son for what they have in common. The nostalgia, the dream, the fragile, anxious, and disturbing need of all human love to endure and not to die has in God the strength and status of an eternal Person;

3. We can speak of a third activity in God. It is the life of God in the souls of those who love him. God has sent his Son. God gives God to men, and he gives himself twice. He has given his Son, but the Son and the Father send their Spirit to make their dwelling in us. The Church calls this most profound aspect of our life "divine missions". God became man so that we could become God. But not in any way at all. Not in the manner of a fusion or a dissolution in the great All, as some nature mystics or, for example, the metaphysics of India propose. For the Christian, it is proposed that he "become god" through a "supernatural" growth of knowledge and of love that God himself offers man on the condition that he disarm himself. This divine "activity" has an

effect distinct from God. Man can make a return or not.
There truly is in this gift a new presence of the Divine
Persons in the human soul.

Imitate God?

Whether man knows it or not, human life, in what ultimately
distinguishes it from that of the animal, is entirely invested in
and sustained and oriented by an imitation of these three
divine activities.

1. We pursue divine creation through our work insofar as
it cooperates in changing the world, work that is achieved in
the outside world. But, in the very achievement of her work,
Thérèse, following Jesus, was aware of imitating the "customs" of God. She did not care about practicing the virtues
only in order to be in accordance with the constitutions
of Carmel or with the *Papier d'exaction* [paper of exaction],
the term designating, according to a literal translation from
Spanish, the booklet that regrouped into about a hundred
pages the exact prescriptions on silence, the horarium, the
way to behave at table, and so forth, left by Teresa of Avila,
the reformer of Carmel, to the first prioresses who founded
the Carmels in France. Thérèse saw farther than this. Which
made her at once much more attentive and much freer. By
applying herself to the moral virtues, she imitated the "customs of God", as Saint Thomas said,[2] which is to say, the great
divine attributes whose splendor she discovered in her biblical
and liturgical reading. By imitating the patience of Jesus, she
participated in the eternity of God; by imitating his chastity,
she participated in the divine immutability; through his humility, she participated in the All-Powerful, and so forth.

[2] Cf. Summa Theologiae Ia, IIae, q. 61, art. 5, et q. 62, art. 1 ad 2um.

2. Thérèse's existence was not limited to this obstacle course. The theological virtues proposed more. The life of knowledge and of love, when it is turned to God and elevated by the gifts of grace and of the Holy Spirit, permits the Christian to enter into the inner secret of God. It is no longer a question merely of imitating the divine ways. Thérèse of Lisieux expressed it very well in the invitation to her veiling, just as she did in her Act of Oblation, and, following her, as Elizabeth of the Trinity did when she asked, in her wonderful prayer, to become "another humanity" for the Word. The expression might make some theologians hesitate. Elizabeth, like Thérèse, was only intuitively echoing the first chapter of the Letter to the Ephesians, so often restated by John of the Cross. There are so many passages from Thérèse's poetry that could be quoted here, passages where she has a rarely equaled, and theologically perfect, boldness, for example, in PN 32: "I have found my Heaven in the Blessed Trinity / That dwells in my heart, my prisoner of love" (PST 154). And in PN 17: "Living on Love is holding You Yourself. / Uncreated Word, Word of my God, / Ah! Divine Jesus, you know I love you. . . ./ In loving you I attract the Father. / My weak heart holds him forever. / O Trinity! You are Prisoner / Of my Love! . . ." (PST 89–90). An extremely rare expression in the history of spirituality, but one that says everything.

3. Thérèse of Lisieux helps to take a further step when she evokes the source of her apostolic and missionary life. Of course she remains enclosed in her Carmel, but what leads her in her monastery to follow Teresa of Avila if not the desire to "save souls and most particularly to pray for priests"? This vocation remains to be explained. How is this to be done? Explicitly and constantly with reference to a trinitarian attraction. Her life was motivated by a communion with the mission of the Word and of the Spirit. The invitation from all

creation to make a return to God implies, indeed, a new presence of the Divine Persons, according to their proper activity,
in the souls of those who are willing to be guided to God.

The Church calls this external effect, distinct but inseparable from participation in the inner life of God, the "visible"
mission of the Word or the Spirit. Thus, Christ knew himself
to be destined to "do the work of his Father"; he came in
order to "bear witness to the Truth". The "invisible" mission
is that which directly coincides with the eternal procession of
the Word. But this mission is indeed followed by an effect,
which is that of the Incarnation, by the whole work of
Christ, by his preaching, starting with his agony when confronted with the rejection of his message ("Will the Son of
Man find faith when he comes to earth again?") up to the
witness of his martyrdom on the Cross and of his attentive
love for each person in his particular destiny, whether it be
a Samaritan, an adulteress, or a betraying apostle. There is
always in Christ a unity between his contemplative life and
his apostolic life, a unity between the invisible and the visible
mission. One could say, in the end, that his whole life is a
passage from an inner mission (his sending by the Father) to
another inner mission (his return to the Father), through the
mediation of an external mission: his Incarnation and his
whole apostolate. This is the very course of the contemplative and apostolic life of Thérèse of Lisieux. This is what
unifies her whole life.

She knew she was invited to both "the table of sinners and
the table of God". She was called to share that third aspect of
divine activity represented by the missions of the Divine
Persons. Just as an external effect corresponds to the sending
of the Son, so missionary concern really implies in a certain
way an external action, a share of work to be performed,
even if one is not destined to preach or to be a missionary: it

would be only through prayer, fidelity, and sacrifices. It was indeed in a trinitarian spirit that Thérèse offered them "to merciful Love".

A very simple example can help us understand this new presence of God. There is something radically new in the heart of a mother and in the heart of her child when the mother teaches her child the Our Father. They are both "transported" into God. There is indeed a new, distinct, external effect in the soul of the child. But this effect, although distinct from the desire of his mother, cannot be dissociated from it. So it is with the sending and the mission of the Holy Spirit. In addition to the external effect, a communion is achieved in the soul, as the Gospel of Saint John says: a "dwelling place" for God. Thérèse's apostolic and missionary concern ends in the birth of a new light on God within her: a communion with the mission of the Word. This is so obvious in the letters she addresses to those she calls her two "spiritual brothers": Father Roulland and Father Bellière, missionaries in Africa and China. With them, she is "transported", and she transports them into God. The "divine missions", according to exact terminology, communicate to the soul a grace that is the image of the characteristic of each Divine Person: the grace of wisdom and of light for the Word, the grace of charity for the Holy Spirit. They end in a new, very real gift of the Divine Person himself. We attain here the most sublime explication of the total unity of Thérèse's hidden life and her apostolic and missionary life and also of the permanence of her influence—witness the incredible fervor that the journey of her relics aroused all over France during the preparation for the centenary of her death. "Where is the wise man. . . . 'What no eye has seen, nor ear heard, nor the heart of man conceived, what God has prepared for those who love him,'

God has revealed to us through the Spirit. For the Spirit searches everything, even the depths of God. . . . No one comprehends the thoughts of God except the Spirit of God" (1 Cor 1:20; 2:9–11).

Thérèse gains access here to the joy proper to all Christian mystery: a share of what serves as the basis for the intimacy of the first two Persons of the Holy Trinity. This is what is best of all, unknown in any human love, that is, that the one engenders the other by loving him. In married love, two beings love each other because they have chosen each other, but the husband is not the son of the wife, and the one the man engenders is never his equal. On the contrary, to the one who is his equal, the man never does anything but communicate gifts; he does not engender her. In God, the engendering of the other is what founds the intimacy. It is not a matter of mere similitude or a mere common possession, but of that absolute identity born of generation. To understand that is to return to the first experience of all life. That is what all love yearns for: to be able to give oneself in such a way to the other that one engenders him, to be able to love the other as he himself is loved. Jacques Maître's book *L'Orpheline de la Bérésina, Thérèse of Lisieux*, in its laborious effort to mobilize the resources of socioanalytical psychology, demonstrates by counterpoint the so much simpler, happier, and more peaceful treasures of trinitarian theology and of the experience of the mystics. What, then, is the "glory" of which Saint Paul speaks, which is shared with us from one degree to the next: "We all, with unveiled face, beholding the glory of the Lord, are being changed into his likeness from one degree of glory to another; for this comes from the Lord who is the Spirit" (2 Cor 3:18), if not the power to love God fully, totally, because he makes it possible for us to love him as he himself is loved? Thérèse saw that in the obscurity of faith, but already on earth as in heaven.

If I Were Queen of Heaven

In the last extant thing written by Thérèse on a little picture, everything is said in one phrase. Thérèse applies to the Virgin that truth of reciprocity which expresses, a fortiori, her primary attitude before God: "O Mary, if I were Queen of Heaven, and you were Thérèse, I would wish to be Thérèse so that you would be Queen of Heaven." This is but an echo of what many saints have expressed; for example, Saint Felicity, when, in her prison, she moaned while giving birth. Her guard called out to her: "If you are moaning now, what will you do when you are between the teeth of the beasts?" Felicity replied immediately through her instinct of reciprocity: "Oh, no, then Another will suffer in me." In the same land of Africa, Saint Augustine wrote: "If, however, as could never be, I were God and you were Augustine, I would wish to become Augustine so that you would be God." This sentence would move Francis de Sales profoundly.

The apostles spent their whole lives feeling Christ's impatience for this mystery to be understood. "You did not choose me, but I chose you. . . . As the Father has loved me, so have I loved you." To know oneself loved and to be happy about it: any psychologist, any "spiritual director", any responsible person, knows the danger incurred by two beings if they express this certitude. Its mere formulation gives substance to what should perhaps not exist. Its mere expression leads to something irreversible, even imprudent or dangerous in human experience. It can lead farther than it should.

To know oneself loved is the single truth that turns a life upside down. It was the certitude that nourished Teresa as she had nourished Saint John. God always takes the first step, not in order to dominate, but to arouse. It is he who has loved us first so that we might respond to him. Everything is said. It is for this that he created us. Thomas Aquinas would sum up the Christian life thus: "Love did not permit God to remain alone." This was the primary truth for Thérèse, who was so taken by the certitude of being loved for herself that she had no fear of regarding her God, her spouse Jesus, as a "beggar" for love.

He Thirsts for Love

God's begging: we should not confuse this intuition with the Nestorian sentiment about the "vulnerability of God" or the recent approximation about the weakness or the suffering of God. No. If God's begging expresses the essence of Christianity, it is in the name of love and of what is the very essence of love in the perfect state: the need for reciprocity.

> See, then, all that Jesus lays claim to from us; He has no need of our works but only of our *love*, for this same God who declares He *has no need to tell us when He is hungry* did not fear *to beg* for a little water from the Samaritan woman. He was thirsty. But when He said "*Give me to drink*," it was the *love* of His poor creature the Creator of the universe was seeking. He was thirsty for love. Ah! I feel it more than ever before, Jesus is *parched*, for He meets only the ungrateful and indifferent among His disciples in the world, and among *His own disciples*, alas, He finds few hearts who surrender to Him without reservations, who understand the real tenderness of His infinite Love. (SS 189 and LT 196)

In 1895 Thérèse wrote: "I have understood more than ever how much Jesus desires to be loved." She had understood it for a long time. But in June 1895, in receiving the inspiration to offer herself to merciful love, she understood "more than ever". It was at the end of this year that she composed her pious recreation *Le Divin Mendiant d'amour* (The divine beggar of love).

*

We do not hesitate to say that the decisive *threshold* of the Christian life is this certitude of being loved, and of being loved in an exceptional way. The word "threshold" must be understood here in the sense of that which orders the whole house, for example, in the country cottages of Haute-Savoie; an opening perfectly oriented toward the sun, protected from the north wind, set on the finest rocks, the threshold opens to the whole house: the common room, the stairs of the barn, the cowshed and the laundry room, the bedrooms. If the threshold is poorly calculated, all the light in the house is diminished. The threshold is that place where one can stand, ever returning to welcome and be welcomed, to rest or to trade.

"So it depends not upon man's will or exertion, but upon God's mercy" (Rom 9:16). "No longer do I call you servants, for the servant does not know what his master is doing; but I have called you friends, for all that I have heard from my Father I have made known to you" (Jn 15:15). This is how Saint Paul and Saint John specified the threshold of Christianity: We are loved and invited to enter into a share of this friendship with God. Now, in itself, love can remain unilateral. That is the point of suffering in all love. Does the other love me as I love him? Why does he not respond? Why his silence? We know what agony this waiting causes, and we also know that, on the other hand, it can be the source of all joy and all happiness for the one who loves.

*

When Christ discarded the idea of servant in order to keep
that of friend, it was indeed to do away with any reason other
than love itself in this sharing. "As I have loved you": This
reciprocity of love between man and God has its origin, its
model, in the inner life of God himself.[3] After Christ, a radical newness has been proposed to man in such a way that he
can no longer explain his destiny to himself by himself alone.
Thérèse understood that it was only on the basis of this reciprocity of love that anything could be illuminated in her life.
It was not because of some work or any good whatever that
Christ loved her, but in virtue of what she was for him. What
the Father said of Christ: "He is my beloved Son in whom I
am well pleased", he wants to repeat about her: "As my Father
has loved me, so I have loved you." Such is the immense
difference, the decisive keystone of the threshold of her life:
to love Christ as someone who expects from her the joy of
being loved. God wanted to do his work in response to his
friends. The episode on which the pastoral charge of Saint
Peter is founded, by the lake after the Resurrection, does not
focus on a call to responsibility, courage, initiative, prospective
intelligence. No, rather it was a call to reciprocity: "Peter, do
you love me?" Three times repeated: "Peter, do you love me
more than these?" (Jn 21:15–17). This was the one certitude
that could establish Peter's life definitively and justify what
follows: "Another will gird you and carry you where you do

[3] For whoever wishes to verify, let us indicate the following texts: (1) The
reciprocity between Christ and his Father, between the Son and the Father: Jn
14:10; 14:13; 15:10; 17:4–5; 17:10. (2) The reciprocity between God and us: Jn
10:27–29; 14:6–7,16–26; 15:15; 16:13. We are given by the Father to the Son,
and it is thus that he receives us: Jn 10:29; 17:6–7, 9, 11–26. The dwelling of
God in us is the fruit of this reciprocity: Jn 10:28–29; 17:24. (3) The reciprocity
between us, which is in the image of that which Christ establishes between
himself and us: Jn 17:11, 21–22; 17:14–16; 17:18; 17:23, 26. Saint Paul picks up
the same idea very forcefully: Col 3:12–13; Eph 4:32; 5:2.

not wish to go" (Jn 21:18). Saint Paul would say it again in the same way: "It is no longer I who live, but Christ who lives in me" (Gal 2:20). "Have this mind among yourselves, which was in Christ Jesus" (Phil 2:5). Many examples of this lived reciprocity in the history of the Church could be given.

Man Proposes, God Disposes?

"For me to love You as You love me, I would have to borrow Your own Love, and then only would I be at rest" (SS 256): Here Thérèse states the ultimate truth of the gospel: God places himself at our disposal; God gives God to men.

For a long time I admired a common inscription in the cottages of Haute-Savoie. On the *bossard*, the beam that supports the ridge purlin, one often finds: "Man proposes, God disposes." I saw it as an act of faith. Certainly. But today the formula does not seem "Christian" to me. One who would dispose, in the sense that we could only submit to it, might be a force; it is not God. I would not want it for a father. A father is the opposite of one who disposes. He is one who arouses, awakens, promotes the freedom and the creation of those to whom he gives life. What good is it to give life if it is not in order to love in the other the difference by which he in his turn is source and love? That is why we must reverse the formula in order for it to be Christian: "God proposes, and man disposes."

Although He Should Kill Me . . .

This is incredible audacity on Thérèse's part. She draws it from her understanding of love:

> You love St. Augustine, Saint Magdalene, these souls to whom "many sins were forgiven because they loved much"

[Lk 7:47]. I love them too, I love their repentance, and especially . . . their loving audacity! When I see Magdalene walking up before the many guests, washing with her tears the feet of her adored Master, . . . I feel that *her heart* has understood the abysses of love and mercy *of the Heart of Jesus*, and, sinner though she is, this Heart of love has not only disposed to pardon her but to lavish on her the blessings of His divine intimacy, to lift her to the highest summits of contemplation.

Ah! dear little Brother, ever since I have been given the grace to understand also the love of the Heart of Jesus, I admit that it has expelled all fear from my heart. The remembrance of my faults humbles me, draws me never to depend on my strength which is only weakness, but this remembrance speaks to me of mercy and love even more.

When we cast our faults with entire filial confidence into the devouring fire of love, how would these not be consumed beyond return? (LT 247, to l'Abbé Bellière, June 21, 1897, GC 2:1133–34)

Thérèse wrote that when she knew herself to be sentenced to death.

In July, in the darkest days of her descent toward death, she would write: "This saying of Job: 'Although he should kill me, I will trust in him' [Job 13:14], has fascinated me from my childhood. But it took me a long time before I was established in this degree of abandonment. Now I am there; God has placed me there. He took me into His arms and placed me there" (LC July 7, no. 3, p. 77). Shortly before her religious profession, at seventeen years of age, she had already expressed this audacity born of reciprocity in one of the most astonishing statements there is: "He will more quickly grow tired of making me wait than I shall grow tired of waiting for Him!" (LT 103, GC 1:612).

To Anticipate the Glory

The understanding of God's begging in the name of the reciprocity of love does not only give Thérèse the audacity of the saints. It unifies her whole life. It is no longer a question for her first of all, or only, of renouncing herself, of observing rules, of making sacrifices, but of responding to the good pleasure of Him who loves her. To know God, to live according to Christ, is to enter into a new order of existence where Another is the center and the light. Few have lived their existence, as Thérèse did, as an anticipation of glory. This is undoubtedly one of the most timely and original things about her witness. And it is not without reason that some of our Orthodox brothers have recognized it. Christ proposes much more than a humanism or an "absolute horizon" for man, much more than a reconstitution, by means of grace, of a lost paradise or of an "integral" human nature. Humanity is invited through faith to something more: to be sons of God— to a new condition, that of a deification.

With the coming of Christ into the world and the accomplishment of the Paschal Mystery, something new has been introduced into the human condition that cannot let itself be defined merely by a morality of grace. Christ and the accomplishment of the Paschal Mystery have brought into the world a new quality of life and introduced a radically new psychology, which is that of glory. By dying on the Cross and in rising again, Christ received the power to communicate this glory not only to his body but to all those who would enter into communion with his present life. That is absolutely new: this participation, in the obscurity of faith, in the life of Christ, eating at the same time "at the table of the Father and at the table of sinners", as Thérèse says. That presupposes a rending, which is itself new in the history of the human psychology, because it partakes of the life of God.

The Mystagogy of Thérèse

One way to avoid being mistaken about Thérèse is to understand the very particular way she approaches the mysteries: always according to what they are for someone else, for Christ, always as the expression of the wishes of someone who loves her, whether it is a matter of prayer, of the Eucharist, of fraternal charity, of institutions, of her vocation, and so forth. All is perceived in terms of exchange, of response, of reciprocity. That changes everything. Hence her frequent reference to "Heaven", not as the object of a future reward, but as the real source of life, here and now—hence the contemporaneousness of her faith: her ultimate reference is glory, Christ living today, in whose existence she participates through faith and who permits her to regard all things as God sees them.

Often, in her poetry, Thérèse says how this real certitude of reciprocity enlivens and transforms all aspects of her life. We can only return to the intuitions of the poems, which are so sound in doctrine. In these poems, which are far from being little diversions, amusements by the good Sister at recreation, Thérèse says, sings, proclaims her most profound feelings. For example, in "Living on Love" (PN 17), "Jesus, My Beloved, Remember" (PN 24), "Heaven for Me" (PN 32), "Saint Cecilia" (PN 3), "The Responses of Saint Agnes" (PN 26), "How I Want to Love" (PN 41), "My Joy" (PN 45), "Why I Love You, O Mary" (PN 54). The edition of the *Complete Works* reveals the true importance of them: beyond the appearance, there, too, is a "trick" of the Holy Spirit. For Thérèse, everything becomes comprehensible only as a response to God:

—Both her vocation: "Opening the Holy Gospels, my eyes fell upon these words: 'And going up a mountain, he called to him men of his own choosing, and they came to him.'. . . This is the mystery of my vocation, my whole life. . . . He does not call those who are worthy but those whom He pleases" (SS 13). "Perfection consists in doing His will, in being what He wills us to be" (SS 14).

—And prayer: "I can't say that I frequently received consolations when making my thanksgivings after Mass; perhaps it is the time when I receive the least. However, I find this very understandable since I have offered myself to Jesus not as one desirous of her own consolation in His visit but simply to please Him who is giving Himself to me" (SS 172).

—Both suffering and fraternal charity. We noted this above, but let us repeat it. She is clear about the duty to love one's neighbor. She knows by heart and quotes the most relevant Gospel texts. She is familiar with disappointment, stemming from herself or from others, when it is necessary to take action. Her hypersensitivity picks up everything: whether from teachers or from her superiors in Carmel, her Sisters, her family. Hence there are the normal temptations to feverish activity or revolt. She explains this herself in chapter 10 of the *Story of a Soul*: Charity has, in an integral way, both the nature of "doing", concrete, practical, demanding, and the nature of a "look", of communion in the look of Christ (cf. SS 120–21). And this communion is primary: it is a matter of responding to the will of another because he loves me, and thus of giving still more value to what I must do because it is he who expects, who begs it of me: "Everything I've done was to give pleasure to God." "I have given him everything. For a long time now, I haven't belonged to myself; I have been surrendered totally to Jesus; he is thus free to do with me what he pleases." At a time when so many Christians

were carefully keeping account of their acts of virtue, hoping
to save up for a reward worthy of their merits, Thérèse loved
gratuitously, squandered, gave with full hands: "When one
loves, one does not calculate." Her whole attitude can be
summed up in this affirmation: "I am not an egoist. It is God
whom I love, not myself." Here is love expressed by the
inspired impulses of a heart worthy of a child, by familiarity
so astonishing and so contrary to the atmosphere of late
nineteenth-century Carmels. Thérèse challenged the fears
that paralyzed her companions: "I do not understand souls
who are afraid of so tender a Friend." "Since he has given me
to understand the love of the heart of Jesus, he has driven all
fear from my heart." "Ah! the Lord is so good for me that it
is impossible for me to fear him." "How do you want me to
fear someone whom I love so much?" Since God is truly her
Father, since she is truly his child, why not call him "Papa"?
"If, through some impossibility, God himself did not see my
good actions, I would in no way be grieved. I love him so
much that I would want to be able to please him even if he
didn't know it was I."

To Remain Free

"To please him": behind this almost childish expression there
is the highest form of abandonment, of trust, and the strongest affirmation of the reality, the immediacy of her faith. It is
for Christ living today, in glory, that Thérèse lives. That
removes none of the violence of the battle, but she wages
combat knowing that the victory is already achieved. That is
why her constant effort will consist of never letting the purity
of her gaze of faith be changed, and to that end, of never
letting the freedom of her heart, the freedom to love, be
weakened, or at least of always recapturing it. It was a matter

everywhere of remaining free in order to be able to recognize Love: behind the face of her father in humiliation (in 1889–1892 especially); behind the maternal face, though often disfigured by jealousy, of her prioress, Marie de Gonzague; behind the still more motherly, but also humiliated, face of Mother Agnès of Jesus, her sister (for example, during her term as prioress between 1893 and 1896: Thérèse had at that time to protect her heart from the normal compassion she might have felt for her sister during scenes made by Mother Marie de Gonzague); behind the humiliated face of another sister, Céline, whom Thérèse considered her other self, almost her child, and whose beginnings in religious life (1894–1897) were somewhat catastrophic, humiliating for Céline and thus for Thérèse.

Throughout all this everyday life, she had to recognize Love, but not any love whatsoever, but rather love whose "characteristic is to abase itself". God does us the honor of sharing the thought of his Son, and henceforth we are invited to look at everything as Christ does. God needs our love as he needs his Son, and this is no longer optional now that he has decided, and he has decided it eternally. We have the very real power to give him to him in ourselves, and if we refuse, there is a gift of the Son to the Father that does not take place, without, however, the eternal gift ever being able to cease. "I have called you friends. . . ." God has only one love, and when he loves, he can give only that. The Father wants to relive with us what takes place between his Son and himself: the gift of his Son to himself; it is this gift that he makes to us: an offering that alone can in the end, with certainty, allow us to glimpse the reason for creation, "the secret hidden from the wise and revealed to little ones".

CHAPTER SEVEN

Victim of Justice or of Love?

Preserved in the Lisieux Carmel, along with other documents of the period, is a circular of a Carmelite in Luçon who died on Good Friday, April 12, 1895 (the text of which is below). The circular is dated May 30, 1895. Thérèse could have heard it read (in the refectory or at recreation) before the Mass of Sunday, June 9; in any case, before the drafting of her Act of Oblation to Merciful Love, recited on June 11, 1895. A comparison of the circular with what Thérèse wrote shows something highly significant: they are complete opposites!

The difference in intuition is not one of "fear" as opposed to "trust"—which is only a consequence. The essence is in what motivates the orientation of their lives. For Thérèse, it was not a matter first of all of paying, of suffering, of making sacrifices, and so on, but of allowing love to respond to love. The following sequence could be worked out to express the entire spirit of her life:

—Love lives by reciprocity; to love is to accept that the One who loves me gives me whatever is necessary to respond to him;

—Thérèse discovered this reciprocity in seeing how much, despite his power, the Other refuses to use the means of power and always presents himself as a "beggar"; then freedom, trust, and thus a victory over all fear can arise;

—That leads her to take the One whom she loves as source and support;

—From which comes the whole orientation of her life: to offer herself in response to this begging for love.

*

In discovering and listening to the warm invitation of Wisdom: "If someone is very little, let him come to me" (Prov 9:4, according to the Vulgate), Thérèse became aware in a much clearer way of the preferential tenderness of God for the weakest and the most impoverished of his children and, thus, of the privilege of the little and the weak. The Father in heaven—Jesus (Thérèse, as we know, went constantly from "God" to "Jesus" and back again)—is Love, and "the nature of love is to humble oneself" (SS 14). A privileged case, Thérèse dares to proclaim: "The weaker one is, without desires or virtues, the more suited one is for the workings of this consuming and transforming Love" (LT 197, GC 2:999); this opening to the "workings" of Love requires conditions, of course, but it has its roots in the exceedingly great love of God faced with the situation of one who wishes to love him infinitely. "In order that Love be fully satisfied, it is necessary that It lower Itself, and that It lower Itself to nothingness and transform this nothingness into *fire*" (SS 195).

It was indeed in the face of the humiliation of God that Thérèse, following Saint Paul and Saint John, became certain of her power, through the grace of God, over the very heart of God, over the very love of God to love him as he himself loves: "O Trinity! You are Prisoner of my Love! . . ." (PN 17: "Living on Love", PST 90); "The favor of flying towards the Sun of Love with the *Divine Eagle's own wings*" (SS 200). Thérèse was only reworking, in a stronger and more simple

way, the same expressions used by her master Saint John of
the Cross when he describes this intoxicating awareness of
being able to give God to God.

But Thérèse, through the little way, perceived very well
that the nature of hope, founded on the reciprocity of love,
offers this possibility to little ones far in advance of the ultimate stage of transforming love.

Thérèse would have exulted if she had found in theologians the reason for which any act accomplished in charity
possesses a completely meritorious value with respect to eternal life and all the increases of love on earth. Saint Thomas
Aquinas expressed the very simple reason for this admirably
well. This act of charity comes not only from human freedom but also, and inextricably, from the grace of the Holy
Spirit. The "meritorious" value of this act corresponds to the
"virtue", the power, the very presence of the Holy Spirit,
who draws man toward eternal life and toward those increases
of love.[1] Thérèse would have been thrilled by this virtual
equality—which will never be anything but virtual—that
theology evokes between the act issuing from created charity,
participation of the Holy Spirit,[2] and the love with which
God loves us.

Let us stress this. We are here at a decisive junction of the
newness of the Gospel, of the most crucial Christian reflection, of the most radical newness that Christianity among all
religions brings, and, it is necessary to recognize, of what is
one of the irreversible and most original characteristics of
the theology and the genius of the anthropology of a Saint
Thomas Aquinas.

It is perhaps useful to point this out to any who might

[1] See, for example, *Summa Theologiae* Ia IIae, q. 114, art. 3, and IIa IIae, q. 24,
art. 6, ad 1 m.
[2] Cf. ibid., IIa IIae, q. 24, art. 7.

wonder if the elevation of Thérèse of Lisieux to the title of
Doctor of the Church is justified. It is once again shining at
the very heart of the essence of her whole message.

The Soul Gives God to God

Thérèse sensed with extraordinary strength and certainty
that God had the ability and the desire both to take possession of man's heart and to give him power over his own
heart in order to accomplish their common dream of love.
The desire of love, the ambition of love can be realized: it
is God who will accomplish it in our heart. With Saint
Thomas, Saint John of the Cross fully confirms Thérèse's
intuitions. Besides, had she not read this page of *The Living
Flame of Love*:

> Being the shadow of God through this substantial transfor-
> mation, it [the soul] performs in this measure in God and
> through God what He through Himself does in it. For the
> will of the two is one will, and thus God's operation and
> the soul's is one. Since God gives Himself with a free and
> gracious will, so too the soul . . . gives to God, God Himself
> in God; and this is a true and complete gift of the soul to
> God. . . . Thus it gives Him to its Beloved, who is the very
> God who gave Himself to it. By this donation it repays God
> for all it owes Him, since it willingly gives as much as it
> receives from Him.
>
> Because the soul in this gift to God offers Him the Holy
> Spirit, with voluntary surrender, as something of its own (so
> that God loves Himself in the Holy Spirit as He deserves), it
> enjoys inestimable delight and fruition, seeing that it gives
> God something of its own which is suited to Him according
> to His infinite being. Although it is true that the soul cannot
> give God again to Himself, since in Himself He is ever Him-
> self, nevertheless it does this truly and perfectly, giving all that

was given it by Him in order to repay love, which is to give as much as is given. . . .

A reciprocal love is thus actually formed between God and the soul, like the marriage union and surrender, in which the goods of both (the divine essence which each possesses freely by reason of the voluntary surrender between them) are possessed by both together. They say to each other what the Son of God spoke to the Father through St. John: *Omnia mea tua sunt et tua mea sunt et clarificatus sum in eis* (All my goods are yours and yours are mine, and I am glorified in them).[3]

It would be difficult to find a better summary of what Thérèse thought and lived of the mystery of God than this page from her Carmelite master. It is enough to compare these lines with the three well-known passages from Thérèse to which we have already alluded: on the one hand, with what she entitled her "Letter of Invitation to the Wedding of Sister Thérèse", on the occasion of her veiling (SS 168–69), then with the note she wore over her heart on the day of her profession, September 8, 1890, and finally with the Act of Oblation to Merciful Love.

Sister Anne-Marie of Luçon

Now we can take a closer look at the essential passages of the circular mentioned above, which was preserved by chance in the archives of Lisieux. This was a death notice for a Carmelite of Luçon. The postmarks make it evident that this was distributed before Sunday, June 9, 1895, the day when Thérèse received during Mass the inspiration to offer herself to merciful love. In this circular it is recalled that Sister Anne-Marie

---

[3] Saint John of the Cross, *Living Flame of Love*, stanza 3, nos. 78–79, in *The Collected Works of St. John of the Cross*, trans. Kieran Kavanaugh, O.C.D., and Otilio Rodriguez, O.C.D. (Washington, D.C.: ICS Publications, 1979), 641.

offered herself to divine "justice". This was indeed what would help Thérèse clarify her thinking. Few pages can help us gain a deeper understanding of Thérèse and her conformity to the great theological and spiritual tradition that we have just recalled. Here, then, is what Thérèse heard read just before she wrote her own Act of Oblation:

> She [Sister Anne-Marie of Luçon] maintained to the end of her life the same ardor for expiation and suffering. All I can say is that our dear departed one ardently desired to prove the glory of God and to save souls. It was to this end that she sought suffering and that she very often offered herself as a victim to divine Justice. To obtain the conversion of one member of her family, she deprived herself completely of fruit for an entire year. In order to convert a poor sinner who had been recommended to her, she resolved not to eat butter, although she liked it very much, for the whole rest of her life. Last July, our good Sister again made her long retreat at the same time as the priests of the diocese, with a new and greater fervor and desire to purify herself more and more of her imperfections so as to go to heaven without passing through Purgatory. After that, this thought scarcely ever left her; in her retreat resolutions, we find the following notes: "Beseech Our Lord to punish me for sin and to make me suffer pain and trials, according to his good pleasure, for the needs of Holy Church and the salvation of souls so as to go, without delay, to bless, adore, love, and glorify God in blessed eternity." Her sufferings were only increased in their intensity, but she endured them with great patience, desiring to suffer even more in order to achieve here on earth the purification of her soul. She wished so ardently to die on Saturday so as to enjoy the privilege of the Sabbatine Bull; we ourselves hope that she was granted her prayer, for she gave her last breath on Friday evening, after first Vespers of Saturday. The great day finally arrived; the day of mercy and of justice, of sadness and of love. All her life she had known scarcely anything but

consolation and the sweetness of love: the time had arrived
to experience the purifying and ever merciful trials. Often,
we caught from her dying lips this cry interrupted by her
agony: "I bear the rigors of Divine Justice . . . Divine Justice . . . Divine Justice! . . . O Jesus!, come, come quickly; I
can no longer. . . I accept the inner torment. . . . The uncertainty . . . the uncertainty. . ." Raising her ice-cold, trembling hands and looking at them, she said: "I do not have
enough merit; I must acquire it." For two to three hours, on
Good Friday, the struggle was terrible; we will hope that our
beloved Sister, so full of confidence in divine mercy, will have
received a favorable reception by the sovereign Judge; but, as
the judgments of the Lord are inscrutable, we beg you please
to add to the prayers already requested.

Several days after having heard or read this death notice,
Thérèse would offer herself, not to Justice, but to merciful
Love. Nothing can be added to what she says there. Only that
all Christians are called to the same response, to the same
reciprocity, even if they do not know it or cannot . . . Thérèse
has definitively recalled that this was not a matter of heroism
but one of trust, open to everyone:

> This year, June 9, the feast of the Holy Trinity, I received the
> grace to understand more than ever before how much Jesus
> desires to be loved.
>
> I was thinking about the souls who offer themselves as
> victims to God's Justice in order to turn away the punish-
> ments reserved to sinners, drawing them upon themselves.
> This offering seemed great and very generous to me, but I
> was far from feeling attracted to making it. From the depths
> of my heart, I cried out:
>
> "O my God! Will Your Justice alone find souls willing to
> immolate themselves as victims? Does not Your *Merciful Love*
> need them too? On every side this love is unknown, rejected;
> those hearts upon whom You would lavish it turn to creatures

seeking happiness from them with their miserable affection; they do this instead of throwing themselves into Your arms and of accepting Your infinite *Love*. O my God! Is Your disdained Love going to remain closed up within Your Heart? It seems to me that if You were to find souls offering themselves as victims of holocaust to Your Love, You would consume them rapidly; it seems to me, too, that You would be happy not to hold back the waves of infinite tenderness within You. If Your Justice loves to release itself, this Justice *which extends only over the earth*, how much more does Your Merciful Love desire to *set souls on fire* since Your Mercy *reaches to the heavens*. O my Jesus, let me be this happy victim; consume Your holocaust with the fire of Your Divine Love! (SS 180–81)

CHAPTER EIGHT

In His Gaze, I Understood All

Thérèse's second attitude before God is inseparable from the first. The desire of love is not only that the other be there as a source, capable of helping us respond. Love does not rest until it has attained its other goal: to be but one with the other. The one who loves has the desire to lose himself in the other, to let the other, to let God do everything in us. The weaker and more impoverished, the poorer and more fragile one of the partners is, the more he calls the other to come into his life, to invade everything.

These are the two desires of love, and there is nothing to be feared in taking them in their strongest sense. It is true that we have to purify our ideas, and Thérèse was a master of purification, in a way that is much more fearsome—and much more gentle and subtle—than any psychoanalyst's. Thérèse took both of these two movements seriously:

The first was the desire to give her Lord love for love, to offer him all the sacrifices possible, to save souls. She says so in her Act of Oblation to Merciful Love, and there it is through reciprocity, through response to the marvels she has discovered and of which she wants to sing.

The other desire was that of being but one with her God, of losing herself in him, of letting him reign within her, for, all alone, she could do nothing. One word sums up this second movement: the choice of mercy. God does everything in order to restore us to the beauty he wants for us so that we might be one with him.

*

Saint Augustine is surprised, in one of his sermons, that the good thief understood the Bible better than the doctors of the Law. And he begins to question the good thief in order to know if, between robberies, he has studied the Scriptures, and how he was able to understand Isaiah 53, whose fulfillment the doctors of the Law were not capable of recognizing, even though it was effected on Calvary right before their eyes and through their own treatment. Why, in order to confess his faith in Christ, did the good thief choose that precise moment when the disciples no longer wanted to believe? And Saint Augustine lends the good thief this single response: "No, I have not studied the Scriptures, but Jesus looked at me, and in his gaze, I understood all." Which we would freely translate: Unless in a certain way one has understood everything before any explanation, one has understood nothing in Christianity.

"Jesus looked at me, and in his gaze I understood all." What Thérèse of Lisieux understood, she summed up in one word. One word that goes back to every one of the great moments of her life. An inexhaustible word: it was totally new, misunderstood, startling at the time of Christ, but it is always difficult to "realize". It cannot be reduced to notions; rather, it leads into life itself, to the heart of God. It has been lived to the point of tears by Christ's partners. It contains the sole reality that can help us go to the depths of ourselves and to the depths of God's secret. It is the supreme reality for Thérèse of Lisieux: mercy.

She opens the story of her life by saying: "I'm going to be doing only one thing: I shall begin to sing what I must sing eternally: '*The Mercies of the Lord*'" (SS 13). She ends this story (Manuscript A) by writing: "How will this 'story...' end? ... I don't know, but what I am certain about is that God's Mercy will accompany her always" (SS 181). And what will the summit of her life be? An act of oblation to merciful love: "May my soul take its flight without any delay into the eternal embrace of *Your Merciful Love*" (SS 277). Finally, when she finds her definitive way, "this vocation that is love", how does she explain it to her older sister, imploring her to understand? "My desires of martyrdom *are nothing*. ... What pleases Him is ... *the blind hope that I have in His mercy*. ... That is my only treasure" (LT 197, GC 2:999). It is clear: her only treasure. "To me He has granted His *infinite Mercy*, and *through it* I contemplate and adore the other divine perfections! All of these perfections appear to be resplendent *with love*; even His Justice ... seems to me clothed in *love*. ... What should I fear then?" (SS 180). The last word of Thérèse's final letter is "He is only love and mercy!" (LT 266, CG 2:1281). At the heart of the Church, the message from Lisieux is one of mercy. Mother Agnès was not mistaken. To the question posed to her during the 1910 process about why she desired the beatification of her sister, she spontaneously gave but one reply: "Because it will procure the glory of God and above all make known his mercy" (PO 134).

*

The notes in the *Manuscrits autobiographiques* of the new centenary edition (NEC) are quite invaluable, for they sum up the treasures discovered during the long years of work that were necessary in order to establish the authentic texts of

Thérèse of Lisieux. We do regret, however, that the note concerning mercy in Ms A 2 r° 6 is content to repeat a few lines, certainly accurate but still very brief, from the edition of Father François de Sainte-Marie. When will mercy cease to be spoken of as a "theme"? For Thérèse, mercy was not only a "theme" but the supreme divine reality. If it is good to recall with Father François de Sainte-Marie that for her it was the "golden key" and the "supreme principle of intelligibility", a little theology is indispensable for entering into Thérèse's thinking. She understood perfectly that mercy was the supreme attribute of God and the only light capable of introducing the mysteries of revelation to everyone. Let us hope that her doctorate will help theologians to adjust fundamentally their way of seeing mercy, for instance, when they interpret Saint Thomas Aquinas as being first of all the doctor of the being of God, even though he is the doctor of redemptive mercy.[1]

When mercy is at issue, its reality is quickly removed by putting it in the department of "themes" or "spirituality", although the very essence of all theology is at stake, or, to repeat Father François' note, the "golden key" and the "supreme principle of intelligibility". If one is content with ready-made ideas about mercy, it is impossible to understand the reason for Christ's coming or the motive of the Incarnation; impossible to respect the intimacy of God's presence to the human being or the Christian and gratuitous quality of grace; impossible to face one's own sin; impossible to understand the sacraments thoroughly as remedies for human fragility; impossible to discover the nobility of a Christian

---

[1] I have often explained this; please refer to *Dieu seul est humain*, chap. 8: "Miséricorde ou Justice", pp. 175–97; *Le Pouvoir du mal*, pp. 91–123 and 228–71; *La Stupeur d'être*, pp. 130–63; *Dieu riche en miséricorde*, introduction to the encyclical of John Paul II, pp. v–xxxii.

anthropology and meaning of man, time, and history; impossible to know how to read the Bible in its fullness and to respect the greatness of God; impossible to reconcile the divine omnipotence and the nearness of infinite love; impossible to believe in a goodness that presided at creation and not be repelled in the face of evil. In the history of Christian thought, Thérèse is one of those who went the farthest. This is not the least of the reasons for elevating her to the rank of doctor of the Church, just as it was one of the principal motives for her canonization. Thérèse is a remarkable "theologian" of mercy.

Compassion or the desire for justice can be rather quick to provoke acts of mercy. These acts can still be done more to liberate the one who performs them than by love of another. It is normal for the one who has received to experience a feeling of indebtedness toward the one who suffers. In God, neither compassion nor justice is the source of mercy, but the Divine Being himself, because he is love, "infinite" love. God alone can "be" mercy. Before saying his personal name to Moses, Yahweh reveals himself as the one "who has seen the misery of his people, who knows their sufferings, their anguish, and has come down to deliver them". In Saint John, the Word of life comes from God his Father in order to bring back to his Father those "who are in shadows". Thérèse understood that in a brilliant way. She understood that the order of things was affected by sin and that, with mercy, love invented a new order. Through sin, we treat God as an "other" whom we would like to dispense with. We place ourselves under the sole demand of justice, which is the virtue of otherness. Thérèse saw that, in a certain way, through mercy, God takes things back again, that he emphasizes and reinvents a new order where love can finally gain the upper hand. Mercy has to do with the very being of God. It is love when he recreates the way in which he will be able to be triumphant. Thérèse insists on this hundreds of times. The single word "mercy" is repeated more than eighty times in her writings. And "love", 756 times. Her thought is very well expressed in the parable, which she creates herself, of the "skillful doctor" (see below, pp. 140–41). Of course, God does not change "because of" sin, but our relations with him are changed by the rupture caused by the fault that turns God away. We know how the reading of Isaiah was a decisive jolt for Thérèse, when she discovered there that "God is like a mother who never stops consoling and caressing her child" (see SS 188). Following the prophets, Thérèse grasped the maternal aspect of divine love. A mother does not forget her infant. The names of his children are inscribed in the palm of his hand. No more than any mother can God bring himself to let the final word be one of rejection, rupture, or revolt. When mercy recreates the order, it reveals at the same time what God holds most closely: love. It is no longer, then, solely a question of the salvation of men but one of God himself. God is stirred for his own good. This is what Scripture means when it speaks of the "entrails" of mercy. Thérèse understood how the tenderness of God might fear being considered other than it is. Evil, weakness, sin itself will paradoxically work toward the ultimate re-creation of the true order of God: the goodness of love.

A Relentless Rejection

The rejection of the idea of mercy has been chronic and relentless. Even in the time of Christ, this idea was so strong, unexpected, and breathtaking that all were tempted to reject it. For each of the classes or sects that claimed to be in possession of the truth, this idea of being led by faith to

receive, to accept a salvation in the very name of one's suffering and poverty was insupportable—both for the Essenes,
monks withdrawn to the desert for whom only flight, separa-
tion from the world to the point of refusing marriage, could
assure a purity worthy of God; and for the zealots, tough,
underground resistance fighters, for whom only political
combat and revolution against the occupying power could
assure the reestablishment of Messianism; and for the Phari-
sees, apostles of a religion for the people, of an adaptation to
the necessities of the world that permitted the drawing up of
a code of prescriptions that one could follow in order to
justify oneself. Whether one flees, revolts, or measures salvation by one's own justice: one no longer needs mercy.

Thérèse said how much she would have loved to know
Hebrew in order to enter more fully into the meaning of the
Gospels. Undoubtedly this would have been a great joy for
her, especially with respect to this subject. Few Hebrew words
are more eloquent through their etymology than these four
words that serve to express the reality of mercy: *hanan*, "to
bend down"; *hamalnoum*, "to suffer with, to spare because
one has pitied"; *raham-rahamin*, "to be gentle, the mother's
breast, the womb, the place that gives life"; *naham*, "to soothe
someone; to make his moaning stop by helping him to
breathe". What a program! For Thérèse, this was the plan
God had with respect to man.

At the Table of the Condemned

In order better to grasp how Thérèse of Lisieux's intuition
placed her on a level with the greatest who have had a sense
of this mystery—Saint Augustine, Thomas Aquinas, Pascal—
let us recall some of the difficulties: those that come from us,
those that come from the Gospel.

From us? Of course, we have ideas about justice and mercy. Very early on, our conscious life having scarcely begun, we have an idea of others. We know very well what it means to have difficulty or to cause harm, and thus we should know what mercy is: a heart that "takes on affliction", a "heart that holds the affliction of the other as his own because he loves". Of course, with some exceptions, all men would like to provide a remedy for affliction, but often this is in the name of compassion or in the name of justice. To do so in the name of mercy poses another question. Buddhists, who have indeed placed compassion at the center of their essential attitude—witness the admirable Amida in the national treasure of Horyu-ji—make manifest the difference between compassion and mercy. The sight of pain is obviously unbearable for everyone. So, since we ourselves do not want to suffer it, we try to soothe the other; and that is indeed compassion, the revolt or the struggle and its commitments, and it is noble. Since we have some good and the other is in a state of want, we feel the injustice of the discrepancy and we act to bring a remedy to it. Once again, this would in itself be a great thing if we were to accomplish it. We can strive toward it, not lay claim to it. Mercy places us in the presence of another abyss: it does indeed spring from a hatred of evil, it *is* a hatred of evil, but it acts through love of the other, without knowing if it will itself be soothed and freed from the weight of the injustice felt or from a compassion that is too heavy.

"To live the misery of the other", as Christ did, to sit at the table of the condemned, among the condemned, an innocent who comes to let himself be accused in order to refrain forever from the power to judge: that goes well beyond justice or compassion. To live the misery of the other as if it were our own because we cannot part with the love that is the sole law of God. This experience eludes us men. Christ and his gaze are necessary for us to understand that it is possible.

*

There is another difficulty. It comes from the Gospel itself. In fact, we encounter there two faces of God: a face of infinite, intimate love, but also a face of justice. A rigorous and strict God, the one we meet, for example, in the Sermon on the Mount: "Make friends quickly with your accuser, while you are going with him to court. . . . [Y]ou will never get out till you have paid the last penny" (Mt 5:25–26). And, on the other hand, this God of incredible goodness, who almost seems blind in the way he erases everything when dealing with the woman caught in adultery, with Zachaeus, with the Samaritan woman, with Peter, who has betrayed, with the good thief . . .

*

So which face do we follow? In order to escape the anxiety, we sidestep, we find a compromise . . . we tone down justice and mercy, one by the other, and in the process we weaken them both. We are tempted to say: "God is just, but that is not so serious since we are told that he is love." At the same time, we imply: "God is merciful, but we don't put too much trust in that, for he is just all the same."

Where, then, is the true face of God?

The Humiliated Face

Thérèse perceived that the question of meaning was comprehensive, and it called for a comprehensive response. Her intuition about mercy corresponds to the abyss experienced in the face of what could be the choice of evil or of rupture. These two abysses are linked: For her, God did not choose "beforehand", "without" her freedom, without an awareness of her incapacity. For her, the true acknowledgment of God is accomplished more in the adoption of certain concrete attitudes than in the affirmation of theoretical principles. It can never be repeated enough: after the Incarnation, these are the practical problems that most genuinely confront the truth of God. Thérèse was extremely clear-sighted about whether her attitudes were sound or "fake". This was often agonizing. "My temptation is despair", said the Curé of Ars.

Let us not forget the difficult conditions in which Thérèse, as a trailblazer, was going to reopen the breach, open her path, her "little way", that of trust in mercy. To the inevitable crush of anguish that seizes anyone faced with his faults and with the future was added, for her, the suffering caused by the poor representation of God she had to endure. We shudder at the Jansenist atmosphere of some of pages she read, for example, in the *Conférences théologiques et spirituelles sur les grandeurs de Dieu* [Theological and spiritual conferences on the grandeurs of God], by Father d'Argentan (a Capuchin of the seventeenth century who, along with admirable passages provided by patristics, went to the limit of terror as well as of love). Mother Agnès was moved by it, but not Thérèse (cf. the difference in their attitudes, LT 94, GC 1:577–78, and n. 5). It was in the midst of tragedy, that of the person she most loved, her father confined in a mental hospital, that Thérèse, two years after her entrance to Carmel, in 1890, read this passage from Isaiah 53 and discovered there the ultimate secret of mercy: the veiled face, the humiliated face of the condemned innocent: Christ. The two images were superimposed on each other for her: Christ and her father. She

remembered—but still without perceiving the full meaning—
her premonitory vision at Les Buissonnets, where the face of
her father had appeared to her covered with an apron. He also
had the habit of covering his head with a handkerchief during his crises. Humiliation and anxiety touched her profoundly—when others made allusions such as "How are the
crazy ones?", "He has been taken to the Bon-Sauveur at
Caen?", or when she asked herself the question: Had he not
fallen ill because she had entered Carmel? She bore the misery of another, of precisely the one she loved most, but she
was not content merely to "endure" it, even with courage;
she "loved" this trial because she discovered the meaning of it
in the "humiliated Face" of Christ.

CHAPTER NINE

We Receive from God
What We Hope For

At the time Thérèse entered the Carmel, Sister Fébronie, at sixty-eight, was generally considered old. Sister Marie of the Angels recounts a conversation between Sister Fébronie and Thérèse, a conversation that might date from the end of 1891, after the retreat given by Father Alexis that was so liberating for Thérèse. Thérèse's reply would be worthy of inclusion among the sayings of the desert fathers.

> One day Sister Thérèse and my Sister Fébronie had a spiritual conversation together in which that venerable Sister, who was a little fearful, gave an excessive defense of the rights of divine justice, and Sister Thérèse, those of infinite mercy. But Sister Thérèse, seeing that she was taking in nothing and still remained fixed in her feelings, ended by saying to her seriously, and we would nearly say divinely: "My Sister, you want God's justice, you shall have God's justice. The soul receives from God exactly what it hopes for." (NPPA)

That is, in one decisive sentence, the most certain, the most theological, the simplest, and most evangelical Christian response, the one that sums up everything: "It is we who decide; it is we who choose"; a response that is at once extremely soothing and very formidable.

121

Soothing, for it depends on us; it is up to us to choose. God has left it up to us.

But also very formidable, and Thérèse makes us take one more step here. In fact, her response includes a second part. Of course, we all believe ourselves ready to choose mercy; we are all "for" it. But to choose mercy is not what we think. We are for mercy to the degree that it suits us. We are always ready to exploit its benefits, to profit from it. Since it seems to enter into our game, we believe we choose it, but then we seek only to utilize it. And Thérèse perceived the misunderstanding: the mercy of God is sweet, certainly, and much sweeter than we think, but it does not play our game as we think. These are the final words she would write in her little notebook, with an exhausted hand, the last lines in pencil to warn us:

> Yes, I feel it; even though I had on my conscience all the sins that can be committed, I would go, my heart broken with sorrow, and throw myself into Jesus' arms, for I know how much He loves the prodigal child who returns to Him. It is not because God, in His anticipating Mercy, has preserved my soul from mortal sin that I go to Him with confidence and love. (SS 259)

It is not for the benefits she had received that Thérèse had confidence. Thérèse had seen the distressing paradox, the very one that was Luther's question, that is, that if we do not love mercy for itself, we do not "choose" it. If we do not want it, independently of the benefits we hope for from it, we discover ourselves to be incapable of choosing it, even in order to be saved, for then we still call for justice. We would like to be able to get away without having to love, without having to yield, without needing to approve, to accept, to delight in this dependence, with a heart that is lost, with respect to God's love.

After her oblation in 1895 to Merciful Love, Thérèse would often return to this point.

One of her favorite novices, Sister Marie of the Trinity, recounts:

> I had an extreme fear of God's judgments, and, despite every-thing Thérèse could say to me, nothing lessened it. One day I posed this objection to her: "We are constantly told that God finds blemishes in his angels; how do you expect me not to tremble, I who am imperfection itself?" She replied to me: "There is only one way to force God not to judge us at all, and that is to go before him with empty hands." "How do we do that?" "It is quite simple", Thérèse replied. "Don't keep anything back; give what you have in the measure you gain it. As for me, if I live till I'm eighty, I will still be just as poor; I don't know how to be economical . . . all that I have, I spend right away to purchase souls. If I were expecting at the mo-ment of death to present little coins and have them judged at their just value, Our Lord would not fail to discover some alloy in them, which I would certainly go to Purgatory to remove." "But", Sister Marie of the Trinity responded, "if God does not judge our good actions, he will judge our bad ones, and then what?" "What are you saying?" Thérèse re-turned. "Our Lord is Justice itself; if he does not judge our good actions, he will not judge our bad ones. For the victims of love, it seems to me that there will be no judgment; but rather that God will hasten to repay with eternal delights his own love that he will see burning in their hearts." (VT 73 [January 1979]: 58–59; cf. SS 180).

"For those who offer themselves to love, it seems to me that there will be no judgment. . . ." Strong minds, intellectu-als, will perhaps be tempted to consider these remarks to be pious words, good for devout Christians or religious. Yet here we have one of the summits of Christian thought and the sole response to the final agony, that of all men, believers or not, in the face of their insufficiencies, weakness, evil. Someone else had said exactly the same thing: "He who believes in him is not condemned" (Jn 3:18). Is Thérèse saying anything different? We are saved—and from this very moment—we "are not condemned", because we believe freely in the promises of God, because we love them in themselves, because we identify with, are taken, magnetized by the source of these promises, who is love, mercy. It is no longer a question of exploiting or utilizing this source in order to receive its fruits: it must be adopted, loved for itself as a reason for living, as one loves a face, the ultimate face of God. There we have the heart of this attitude that saves in and of itself, of which Scripture speaks and which is trust, faith in the one who loves us, trust to the end.

Only faith and trust save. But they do not excuse us from being good (as Luther was tempted to think). For they can be born in us only from a goodness more profound than we are: that which consists in sensing the tenderness of God, because we are already taken, bathed, baptized, invested with this tenderness, this grace.

If we fall while persevering in love to the point where the soul can no longer hold back the cry: "My God, why have you abandoned me?", if we remain at this point without ceasing to love, we end by touching something that is no longer misfortune or joy, something that is the central, essential, pure, imperceptible essence, common to both joy and suffering, and that is the very love of God.

CHAPTER TEN

My First Child

The Murderer of the Century

On September 1, 1887, in the calm summer of the little house Les Buissonnets, Thérèse anxiously opened the journal *La Croix* and found there one of the decisive signs of her life.

> The sinister blackguard who murdered the three victims of the Rue Montaigne was executed this morning, and with him ends the vile scandal of recent days. At a very early hour crowds overran the Roquette Plaza and neighboring streets. At 11:30 detachments of the republican guard, on horseback and foot, and the Seine police came to take their place on the plaza. At precisely 3:00 the venerable Abbé Faure arrived, in carriage no. 3751, drawn by a white horse. He was followed closely by MM. Athalin, the examining magistrate, Taylor, head of the Sûreté [criminal investigation department], Garon, second in command, and Martigny, secretary. At 4:45, M. Bauquesne, director of the Roquette, M. Baron, police commissioner, his secretary, and M. Faure went for the first time to cell no. 2, occupied by the condemned. M. Caubet accompanied these gentlemen.
>
> Pranzini slept soundly. M. Bauquesne shook him twice to wake him up. The assassin of Marie Regnaud sat up on his bed, cast haggard eyes all around him, and uttered a hoarse cry. What an awakening! In reality, the miserable one had

not ceased to rely on his pardon. He made violent efforts to speak a little. "You are going to commit a crime. I am innocent!" And he added, making a violent effort to appear calm: "The only thing I regret is not having been able to kiss my mother." In a few seconds, his face became livid. "Courage, Pranzini", M. Bauquesne said to him. "Your crime was too great; M. the President of the Republic was not able to grant you a pardon. Die a good death, and redeem your fault that way." "I am innocent! I am innocent!" he screamed. The two Sûreté agents passed him his boots. He put them on slowly, while the clerk read the sentence. He dressed while trembling, mumbling incoherent phrases. Then he asked for some cold water in order to wash his face and hands. The chaplain, M. Faure, then remained next to him for a few moments. He said to him: "I will be as calm as you, for I die innocent." Finally, he was led to the clerk's office, where Deibler and his assistants had been waiting for several minutes for him to be delivered to them. There, they cut his hair, cut out the neck of his shirt, bound him hand and foot, and, at two minutes to five, while the birds were singing in the trees of the plaza, while a confused murmur arose from the crowd, the command "saber in hand" rang out, a clinking of iron resounded, swords shone, and on the threshold of the prison, whose door opened, the murderer appeared, livid. The chaplain placed himself in front of him to hide the sinister machine from him. The assistants supported him. He pushed away both the priest and the executioners. There he was before the bascule. Deibler pushed him and threw him onto it. One assistant, placed on the other side, grabbed his head, brought it under the blade, holding it by the hair.

But before this movement could be produced, perhaps a flash of repentance crossed his conscience. He asked the chaplain for his crucifix. He kissed it twice. And when the blade fell, when one of the assistants seized the detached head by an ear, let us say to ourselves that if human justice is satisfied, perhaps this final kiss will also have satisfied divine justice, which asks above all for repentance.[1]

That is exactly what Thérèse read that day. She was fourteen years old at the time. In 1895, eight years later, Thérèse remembered it and made this episode an essential moment of her life when she wrote her autobiography and went so far as to speak of the murderer Pranzini as her "first child".

My First Child

"I heard talk of a great criminal just condemned to death for some horrible crimes; everything pointed to the fact that he would die impenitent. I wanted at all costs to prevent him from falling into hell, and to attain my purpose I employed every means imaginable" (SS 99). So Thérèse must have heard talk of the murderer. She was truly going to take charge of him. It was because Pranzini was condemned to death, because he was going to be executed and did not seem repentant, that she was going to make use of everything in order to save him. From that date on, Thérèse consulted *La Croix* to look for a "sign" (SS 100) of the prisoner's conversion.[2]

Finally, on September 1, she discovered the article just quoted. "Pranzini had not gone to confession. He had mounted the scaffold and was preparing to place his head in the formidable opening, when suddenly, seized by an inspiration, he turned, took hold of the crucifix the priest was holding out to him and *kissed the sacred wounds three times!*" (SS 100). Thérèse comments:

[1] *La Croix*, August 31, 1887.
[2] Cf. the perfectly accurate study by Father Guy Gaucher, "Thérèse Martin et l'affaire Pranzini", VT 48 (October 1972): 275–86, which we quote here.

I had obtained the "sign" I requested, and this sign was a perfect replica of the grace Jesus had given me when He attracted me to pray for sinners. Wasn't it before the *wounds of Jesus*, when seeing His divine *blood* flowing, that thirst for souls had entered my heart? I wished to give them this *immaculate blood* to drink, this blood which was to purify them from their stains, and the lips of my *"first child"* were pressed to the sacred wounds! What an unspeakably sweet response! (SS 100).

For Thérèse, her vocation depended on it. This sign was to direct her toward Carmel. "After this unique grace my desire to save souls grew each day, and I seemed to hear Jesus say to me what He said to the Samaritan woman: '*Give me to drink!*' " (SS 100–101).

Let us follow, then, the account by Guy Gaucher:

On March 20, 1887, the lifeless bodies of Régine de Montille, Annette Grémeret, her chambermaid, and that of a little girl of twelve years, Marie (in reality, the daughter of Régine, who made her pass for the daughter of her servant) were found in Paris at 17, rue Montaigne (now called avenue Matignon). The throats of all three had been savagely cut; the jewels of the mistress had disappeared. The real name of Mme. Régine de Montille was Marie Regnaud. Beautiful, she had been seduced at a very young age and abandoned in the capital city. The comte de Montille noticed her there. She was seen in every social gathering of fashionable Paris, which was trying to forget 1870 and the Commune. And a good girl besides, playful, watching over her child. . . . This triple crime caused enormous reverberations as much because of the personality of the victim as of the conditions in which it was committed. All the newspapers the next day related the triple murder on the rue Montaigne with a wealth of horrible details that were to make this crime a subject of unprecedented sales. It must be admitted that there was much here

to entice the public: a sinner of great beauty, a servant devoted to the point of death, and the lamb of sacrifice: the
little Marie Grémeret, to say nothing yet of the guilty party,
who could only be a splendid beast. [3]

Like Being in the Theatre

When he was brought by the Marseille police to Paris, they
did not want to have him get out at the Lyons station, where
a crowd was waiting for him—not to lynch him; rather the
women in it were numerous, "the first sign of the wholly
feminine infatuation that would make this executioner of
women legendary".[4] From Charenton on, Pranzini thus came
into Paris in a convoy of five carriages. His trial opened
before

> a packed room, where only the bearers of a special card
> signed by the president could enter. Mr. Onfroy de Bréville
> was besieged by too many fashionable ladies, and the appear-
> ance of the court of assizes showed the effects of it in a
> shocking way: it was like being in a theatre, or rather at the
> horse races, for the summer day (Saturday, July 9) was radiant,
> authorizing white veil, parasol, and fan. Even in the hands of
> women, lorgnettes were pointed in the direction of the ac-
> cused. The presiding judge felt the effects of it. He had to
> impose silence on these worldly gossipers.[5]

The address to the court by M. Demange, Pranzini's attorney,
brought applause from the room. A noisy show, with the
repeated cry of "Cassation! Cassation!", marked the transfer
of Pranzini to the Grande-Roquette. They were selling his
photograph, a poster that recounted his story, on the streets.

[3] Ibid., p. 276.
[4] Paul Lorenz, *L'Affaire Pranzini* (Paris: Presses de la Cité, 1971), p. 105.
[5] Ibid., p. 184.

"Of all the letters, in very great number, that actually arrived addressed to him, often accompanied by chocolate and cigarettes, only those from his mother were delivered." [6] Finally, after a reprieve was rejected by Jules Grévy, president of the Republic,

> a veritable riot stormed the walls of the Grande-Roquette. At nightfall, at a signal given by some unknown person, everyone joined together as a mob to march toward the prison. Women in plumed hats got down from carriages stopped in a long line on the boulevard Voltaire, advancing side by side with red scarfs and bareheaded girls. Such unison, which made one believe in the end of a society, had never been seen before. And this heterogeneous crowd, pressing toward the plaza where the guillotine was, was demanding Pranzini's reprieve. [7]

I Reproached Myself for My Intoxication

In his book *L'Exécution*, Robert Badinter recalls his arrival in Troyes at the time when he came to litigate one of the last trials to end in the imposition of the death penalty.

In 1972, wild with despair, Buffet and Bontems had shut themselves into the infirmary of the Clairvaux prison and had taken as hostages before slitting their throats an infirmarian and a guard, both of whom had families. This was not just one event among a variety of others. Bontems had a photograph of Thérèse of Lisieux, and the Carmel was praying for him. Now the same crowd that cried "Cassation" for Pranzini cried "Death" for Buffet and Bontems. Few accounts can do as much to give an insight into the atmosphere that surrounded the trial and execution of Pranzini, which

[6] Ibid., p. 243.
[7] Ibid., p. 244.

were so decisive in leading Thérèse to her intuition about mercy.

I knew that they had arrived at the Palace. A long clamor for "Death!" had been raised in the street at the passing of the barred police wagon, which looked like a hearse for the poor. These were the ones they were waiting for, like one waits for the bull to come out into the arena. But it was not joyful impatience or restiveness that animated the public. Hatred and fear wove around this empty box a web of invisible mesh. The court appeared: "Guards, have the accused enter!" An immense sigh arose from the room. These, then, were the ones, the Clairvaux murderers.[8]

The trial was everywhere. Displayed on kiosks, relayed by mail, enlivening all conversation. I walked into the city. I felt it present in each inhabitant. I reproached myself for my intoxication. I entered the first café I came to. At the bar, it was not a question merely of the trial, but rather of its pointlessness. In a definitive tone, accompanied with gestures, one customer threw out to unanimous approval: "With people like that, I would have executed them for you without a trial—quickly done, well done. And that's it!" That is popular justice. All the rest is chatter.

The head warden was waiting for me in the rotunda. He questioned me: "Well, *Maître*, how did you find him?" "Well, yes, he is well." The head warden added, as if to himself, "If only he slept at night. You know, he never stops smoking, one cigarette after another. He's like Buffet. He goes around and around his cell. He doesn't stop till morning." I listened to him. He himself was without any hatred against the assassins of Clairvaux. Thus anything was possible, I thought, if they were pardoned.[9]

[8] R. Badinter, *L'Exécution* (Paris: Grasset, 1973), pp. 83–84.
[9] Ibid., pp. 77–78.

The Face of Hatred

I had seen, as never before, the face of hatred laid bare. And
hatred had gained the upper hand. I was familiar with the
traits of hatred. But it puts on its worst face when it adorns
itself with the mask of justice. Furious hatred is frightening.
But hatred as a dispenser of justice is shameful. I can still see
the raised fists, the snarling grins of the crowd that surrounded that girl with the closely cropped head whom two
men, armed and self-important, led half-naked through the
streets of the city because she was a "Kraut's daughter". Hatred, moreover, always gives even the worst criminal an unexpected dignity. One forgets the guilty one in seeing only the
hunted, wretched being. Mauriac recalled that young hood-
lum who had killed an old woman in order to rob her. When
they were reconstructing the crime, he crossed through the
crowds between policemen. Beneath the blows, the insults,
the spitting, his face had become that of Christ. Those who
are carried away by hatred do not know what a gift they make
to the very object of their hatred.

But hatred makes one doubt everything, and first of all
the justice that hatred applauds. I was still listening to the
clamor, the applause that greeted the condemnation to death
of Buffet and Bontems. The president could ring his bell.
The hunt had come to an end. The beasts were caught. No
doubt the crowd would have applauded if the executioner
had presented it with two heads. And yet, in times past,
when Gilles de Rais, the worst of all criminals, was on his
way to the stake, each one along the way knelt down to ask
God to have mercy on the soul of the sinner. Buffet was not
Gilles de Rais, far from it. Was there anyone among those
who did not know him who implored the grace of God for
this murderer who wanted so much to die? I hope so. I want
to believe so. But I did not meet him in that crowd gathered
around the Palace.

Nothing could change the fact that we had confronted hatred and that it had carried us away.[10]

This testimony makes us recall a tragic incident that took place before the death penalty was suppressed. Despite the fact that, as the lawyer recalls, one of the two condemned had not committed murder, they were both executed. It forces us to enter into the encounter between Thérèse and justice, prayer, and mercy, such as she experienced it with the Pranzini affair. And remember: Thérèse's photograph was in Bontems' cell. In his defense speech for Buffet, who had done everything possible in order not to be pardoned, the lawyer had cried out: "Was there anyone who implored the grace of God for this murderer who wanted so much to die?" One reply was given: the Carmel of Lisieux was praying with Bontems, and Bontems knew it.

The Image of the Crucified

Let us resume Guy Gaucher's account:

> In this Pranzini tragedy, everything would have repelled Thérèse: the savage murders, the sexual excesses of the victim and her murderer, greed, the sordid context (if she had known those details). At the time, they spoke only of the "sinister blackguard", the "monster", the "vile brute". For her, he was "the poor unfortunate Pranzini", and she adopted him as her "first child"! The impulse that carried her toward him was not at all like that disordered attraction of women who threw kisses to the famous womanizer. She went toward him with an evangelical simplicity.
>
> The image of the Crucified revealed to the young girl her missionary vocation; the encounter with Pranzini occurred at that moment.

[10] Ibid., pp. 166–68.

It was not to protest against her surroundings that she went toward the criminal. She was carried solely by the saving love of Christ that she had just discovered. Pranzini was the living experience of it. That does not rule out the possibility that grace was acting in a concrete being; she was at that time at her physical and spiritual peak: her femininity was not absent from this impulse toward Pranzini at the very moment when her vocation of spiritual motherhood was inscribed in her forever. Let us add that Thérèse never forgot her "child", even if his name is never again mentioned in her writings up to the time she died. She shared this secret only with Céline. In Carmel, she would continue to have Masses said for Pranzini. Céline would testify at the process: "The Servant of God called Pranzini her 'child'. Later, in Carmel, when money was put at her disposal for her feast days, she obtained permission from our mother prioress to use it to have a Mass celebrated, and she whispered to me: 'It's for my child; after the tricks he played, he must have need of it! . . . I must not abandon him now.'" (PO 1745)

As at another time, in 1887, she feared "being obliged to say [that the Masses were] for Pranzini" (SS 99).

Let us quote Marcel Moré, who gave an excellent commentary on these statements: "Such a playful tone for Thérèse to use in speaking of a man who had killed three people! Clearly this was a way of hiding a secret that she held close to her heart. . . . The memory of that murderer seems scarcely to have left her mind. Besides, how could a woman forget her firstborn, especially when she had given birth to him in the light of grace? It is only too obvious that between the year 1887, marked by the 'crime' of Pranzini, and the year 1897, when, on her deathbed, she dropped *ex abrupto* that very word 'crime' in front of her sister, who must have been quite surprised by it, she had kept, faithfully shut up in the deepest part of her heart, the image of Pranzini. When she protested 'If I had committed all possible crimes . . .' [LC July 11, no. 6,

p. 89], she freed herself of a silence of ten years, interrupted only by the writing of her autobiography. All possible crimes! Undoubtedly they were, in her eyes, in a general way, all the crimes of humanity, but it is no less certain that, in a much more concrete way, they were those of Pranzini." [11]

Yes, Pranzini played an important role in the life of Thérèse, well beyond 1887. The murderer of the century, the one who could benefit from Mercy like the good thief, put the young girl on the path of the essential. Yes, criminals and prostitutes are called to believe boldly in Merciful Love, for Jesus did not come to call the just but sinners. In a milieu where a murderer was nothing but a monster destined for the guillotine, a child rediscovered the spirit of the gospel. [12]

Thérèse Insensible to the Problems of Her Times?

It has too often been written and repeated that Thérèse lived in a closed circle unaware of the sounds of the world and its problems. One ends up thinking of the saint of Lisieux as not having been of her own time but rather as being timeless. Once again the image of Épinal has prevailed over reality. May it suffice here to outline a few suggestions:

—Thérèse and Pranzini: The question has not been thoroughly explored, although set in place since Marcel Moré.

—Thérèse and Hyacinthe Loyson: The former Carmelite friar and preacher at Notre-Dame de Paris, married and founder of a church, was very much in the news. Thérèse never stopped interceding for him and offered her last Communion on his behalf (cf. LC 157 and LT 129, GC 2:728–29).

—Thérèse and Henry Chéron: Still a child, she had met in the Guérin pharmacy, where he was working, the man who would become mayor, member of Parliament, and minister, a

[11] Marcel Moré, "Crime et sainteté", *Dieu vivant* 14 (1949): 37–71.
[12] Gaucher, "Pranzini Affair", pp. 282–83.

famous anticlerical leader of those "materialists" against
whom her uncle Guérin fought and for whom Thérèse
prayed and offered her life.

—Thérèse and Léo Taxil: The impostor of the century,
author of anticlerical pamphlets, who fooled Catholic opinion through a false conversion before unmasking himself on
April 19, 1897 (cf. DE 187). Thérèse had written to Diana
Vaughan, the convert invented by Léo Taxil. Proceeding with
the imposture, "Diana" responded to Thérèse.

Insensible to the problems of her times, Thérèse? These
four monographs would prove the passionate interest she took
in contemporary questions, those at least that concerned man
in the depths of his being. Through an intuition of the heart,
the saint of Lisieux grasped that Jesus lived among sinners in
order to save them. She did not enter Carmel in order to
separate herself from them, to "protect" herself from contact
with them, but for them, by burying herself in silence, prayer,
a martyrdom of love to the point of sitting at their table and
sharing with them there the bread of sorrow (SS 212).[13]

[13] Ibid., p. 284.

CHAPTER ELEVEN

To Save Sinners by Sinners

Thérèse uses the expression "bread of sorrow" to indicate the meaning of the Christian doctrine of reparation. For her, this doctrine was true, and there was no question of minimizing it. It is so essential to Christianity that without it there would be nothing left, since our entire salvation is the fruit of reparation: that of Christ. We have tried, following Saint Thomas Aquinas, to explain the profound meaning of this in the book *Peut-on éviter Jésus-Christ?* [1] One cannot, on this point of doctrine, remain on the level of elementary ideas or outdated hymns.

"Surely he has borne our griefs and carried our sorrows. ... He was wounded for our transgressions, he was bruised for our iniquities; upon him was the chastisement that made us whole, and with his stripes we are healed" (Is 53:4–5). "Having canceled the bond which stood against us with its legal demands; this he set aside, nailing it to the cross" (Col 2:14).

By inviting us to the banquet of divine life, and in virtue of the very love that made him mount the Cross, God calls us to participate in the reparation itself, by completing what was

[1] Bernard Bro, *Peut-on éviter Jésus-Christ?* (Paris: Éd. de Fallois, 1995), chap. 27, pp. 182ff.

lacking in the Passion of his Son. One can feel weak in the face of such a perspective, but that is to misunderstand it, since God offers it in order to give more, not in order to demand more. He wanted and wants "to save sinners by sinners" so that sinners share in all the privileges of innocence, including that one. This doctrine of reparation affirms, to the contrary, that the saved one is not apart from the Savior, but that he is saved to the point of being invited to become a savior. In Christianity, one does not save by building on the fruits of the Redemption but by participating in the Redemption itself, which is the reparation of a broken love. Whatever one might say, there is a debt to pay, but far from being against love, this demand stems from love itself. What mends love and reconciles those who have ruptured it is crying together over the evil that has been done; those are the tears poured over that very rupture.

Who, after Christ, could claim to have been more grieved by evil than was the Virgin Mary? And yet was she not preserved, absolutely, from all sin?

If we want to enter into something besides a vague dialogue with God, we cannot refuse to contemplate, at least to some extent, what that in fact entails: God leaves us free to want to be separated from him. God wanted to communicate to us a divine privilege, his privilege: the absolute power to choose, but with the risk of becoming our own gods. And we can say that "in heaven" there will be an eternal, divine reward for those who agree to live this privilege in union with God and renounce living alone that power by which we are like him, having thus constructed their freedom through love of the love of God.

Concretely, it is in discovering that we have a positive power of goodness and salvation and that we are with Christ on the side of the Redemption (which can, alone, tap all our forces) that we find a living "solution" to our anguish. We do not "see", but we are certain of acting in an eternally efficacious way. The consequence of refusal remains God's secret: the Church canonizes; she has never condemned anyone. We must understand once and for all that we have nothing less to hope for from God than God. But we must simply know that the hypothesis that would suppress hell risks, like anemia, emptying the Cross of Christ of all its substance. Even without theology, those who are caught up by the love of God know that from experience.

After having discovered the difficulties of our vocation and our freedom, and their possible loss, we must learn to go to God no longer in innocence and despite failures, but precisely as a sinner and by relying on our very distress, that is to say, on mercy.

What God manifests then is that he is love at a depth we had not suspected, the evidence of which appears as a definitive response to all the questions of the Christian life. It is only then that fraternal charity takes on its properly mystical (which is to say, strictly Christian) dimension.

We learn pity only through our own wounds. "After the Resurrection", Pascal said, "Jesus no longer wanted to be touched except through his wounds." The pity and wounds of Thérèse did not need to come from her sin. Lucidity, awareness of her fragility, the hardness of life were enough. The humiliation of her father, his illness, these were her losses, her impetus, her struggle . . .

Now out of all that she draws three movements:

—before God, the assurance of an absolute audacity;

—before her community and her "brothers", an ever-renewed understanding, a rejection of all dialectics;

—before herself, the rejection of all distaste.

1. *A Loving Audacity*

It is impossible not to cite here the parable of the two children and the skillful doctor. Once again, under a banal appearance, Thérèse expresses herself wonderfully well. No page of the spiritual tradition of Christianity has more briefly explained how it is possible to understand mercy when one discovers oneself the object of mercy. We are here at the very threshold of the mystery of the Immaculate Conception, more sensitive to evil than any creature because preserved from evil, through mercy. Thérèse has the audacity to compare herself to Augustine and Mary Magdalen . . .

> Ah! I feel it! Jesus knew I was too feeble to be exposed to temptation; perhaps I would have allowed myself to be burned entirely by the *misleading light* had I seen it shining in my eyes. It was not so for me, for I encountered only bitterness where stronger souls met with joy, and they detached themselves from it through fidelity. I have no merit at all, then, in not having given myself up to the love of creatures. I was preserved from it only through God's mercy!
>
> I know that without Him, I could have fallen as low as St. Mary Magdalene, and the profound words of Our Lord to Simon resound with a great sweetness in my soul. I know that "*he to whom less is forgiven,* LOVES *less,*" but I also know that Jesus has *forgiven me more* than *St. Mary Magdalene* since He forgave me *in advance* by preventing me from falling. Ah! I wish I could explain what I feel. Here is an example which will express my thought at least a little. Suppose a clever physician's child meets with a stone in his path which causes him to fall and break a limb. His father comes to him immediately, picks him up lovingly, takes care of his hurt, using all the resources of his profession for this. His child, completely cured, shows his gratitude. This child is no doubt right in loving his father! But I am going to make another compari-

son. The father, knowing there is a stone in his child's way, hastens ahead of him and removes it but without anyone's seeing him do it. Certainly, this child, the object of his father's tender foresight, but UNAWARE of the misfortune from which he was delivered by him, will not thank him and *will love him less* than if he had been cured by him. But if he should come to learn the danger from which he escaped, *will he not love his father more?* Well, I am this child, the object of the *foreseeing love of a Father* who has not sent His Word to save the *just*, but *sinners*. He wants me to *love* Him because He *has forgiven* me not much but ALL. He has not expected me to *love Him much* like Mary Magdalene, but He has willed that I KNOW how He has loved me with a love *of unspeakable foresight* in order that now I may love Him unto *folly!* (SS 83–84)

I don't hasten to the first place but to the last; rather than advance like the Pharisee, I repeat, filled with confidence, the publican's humble prayer. Most of all I imitate the conduct of Magdalene; her astonishing or rather her loving audacity which charms the Heart of Jesus also attracts my own. Yes, I feel it; even though I had on my conscience all the sins that can be committed, I would go, my heart broken with sorrow, and throw myself into Jesus' arms, for I know how much He loves the prodigal child who returns to Him. It is not because God, in His anticipating Mercy, has preserved my soul from mortal sin that I go to Him with confidence and love. (SS 258–59)

She said to me: "Does a father scold his child when he admits his fault; does he inflict some punishment on him? No, of course not; rather he presses him to his heart."

To illustrate this thought, she reminded me of a story we had read when we were children: a king, during a hunt, was pursuing a white rabbit that his dogs were about to reach, when the little rabbit, sensing that he was lost, quickly turned back on the road and leapt into the arms of the hunter. The latter, touched by so much trust, didn't want to be separated from the white rabbit, not letting anyone touch it, feeding and caring for it himself. "That is what God will do with us", she told me, "if, pursued by justice, symbolized by the dogs, we seek refuge in the very arms of our Judge." (CSG 52)

To a missionary in Tonkin:

I do not understand, Brother, how you seem to doubt your immediate entrance into heaven if the infidels were to take your life. I know one must be very pure to appear before the God of all Holiness, but I know, too, that the Lord is infinitely just; and it is this justice which frightens so many souls that is the object of my joy and confidence. To be just is not only to exercise severity in order to punish the guilty; it is also to recognize right intentions and to reward virtue. I expect as much from God's justice as from His mercy. It is because He is just that "He is compassionate and filled with gentleness, slow to punish, and abundant in mercy, for He knows our frailty, He remembers we are only dust. As a father has tenderness for his children, so the Lord has compassion on us" [Ps 102:8, 14, 13]!! . . . How would He allow Himself to be overcome in generosity? . . .

This is, Brother, what I think of God's justice; my way is all confidence and love. I do not understand souls who fear a Friend so tender. At times, when I am reading certain spiritual treatises in which perfection is shown through a thousand obstacles, surrounded by a crowd of illusions, my poor little mind quickly tires; I close the learned book that is breaking my head and drying up my heart, and I take up Holy Scripture. Then all seems luminous to me; a single word uncovers for my soul infinite horizons, perfection seems simple to me, I see it is sufficient to recognize one's nothingness and to abandon oneself as a child into God's arms. Leaving to great souls, to great minds the beautiful books I cannot understand, much less put into practice, I rejoice at being little since children alone and those who resemble them will be admitted to the heavenly banquet [Mt 19:14; Mk 10:14; Lk 17:16]. I am very happy there are many mansions in God's kingdom [Jn 14:2], for if there were only the one whose description and road seem incomprehensible to me, I would not be able to enter there. (LT 226, to P. Rolland, May 9, 1897, GC 2:1093–94)

A "loving audacity" . . .

2. To Reject Dialectics

It is impossible to express solely through ideas the true conversion implied by mercy. It is a matter of a concrete choice. So it cannot be transcribed in a satisfactory manner solely through abstract notions. Christ gave but a single sign that can indicate that this decision has been achieved: Has one been merciful oneself? It is clear and precise: "Blessed are the merciful, for they shall obtain mercy."

The facts cited above on silence and the greatness of the commonplace in the life of Thérèse of Lisieux are sufficiently eloquent. With others, Thérèse was not content to escape behind the usual subterfuge: since it is difficult to be for the good, for one does not know where that might lead, one can at least agree to be against evil. The latter would be, more or less, the evil of others' faults. Once again, this is the usual method, for example, in politics. It is too easy. One does not shift the responsibility for evil through a dialectic that opposes others. Evil is not to be reduced to ideas any more than to making others feel guilty. That does not mean that mercy is only compassion and remains only on the level of sentiment. Here we have one of the fundamental points of all true ecumenism, beginning with Buddhism and Islam. Thérèse helps us to understand in what the Christian newness of mercy consists.

Mercy is indeed a hatred of evil. It is precisely here that it is dangerous, for this hatred is conducted in the name of a love. The very etymology of the French word *miséri-corde* is precise: it is the heart [*coeur*] that takes on the misery of the other, of the one who is on our path, the one closest to us, the one from whom we would rather turn away in order not to see him. "Grace, like love, is new every morning", said Cardinal Newman. So, too, is mercy, which presupposes a re-creation of motives, decisions, commitments in order to love others. There is no need to search elsewhere for a starting point for Christian "commitment", even political.

Ceaselessly to recreate love and the reasons to love others: that is what Thérèse did while taking advantage of small occasions. That is why she could testify with such certitude of having received mercy in her turn: because she truly "chose" it.

Beyond Distaste

It is another sign that proves we have admitted mercy into our life. It deceives no more. This is no longer a matter of being before God and his gratuitousness but rather of confronting ourselves and disgust itself. It is a certain way of leading one's life, bearing its hope or its failure.

There is in fact a paradox in the gospel. To be his disciples, Christ calls, not the complacent, the soft, the self-satisfied, but warriors. "God has given me the grace not to fear the battle", Thérèse wrote on the threshold of her agony (SS 240). "If anyone loves his father or his mother more than me, he is unworthy of me", and so on. Each beatitude is a call to combat. That seems difficult, impossible to us, and we retreat in fear.

But that is because we listen to these calls that we receive with the implications of our heart, of our heart that is still too hard. They cause us fear insofar as we have not chosen and opted for mercy to the end. What does this mean? We understand, in fact, "Whoever wants to be my disciple, may he carry his cross gloriously, may he carry his cross untiringly, may he carry his cross courageously, perfectly . . ." And that is not possible. But to meet the God of mercy, that is something else. It does not mean the need to feel assured because we are courageous and glorious by ourselves. No. It means those other calls of Christ: "If you are tired and weary, come to me; if you are meek and humble of heart; if you have become like children again, then you will be my disciples. It is for the lost sheep that I have come; it is not the righteous whom I have come to call . . ." Then the one who wants to be my disciple, yes, he will carry his cross. But he will be spared fear if he knows, if he admits, that he carries it "lamentably", as he can, putting up with himself, very often dragging himself. "To carry our cross weakly", Thérèse would say (cf. three letters: LT 81, GC 1:529; LT 82, GC 1:537; and LT 213, GC 2:1042). To love mercy is to accept carrying our life and our cross miserably. Only then do we know that we have not cheated, that we have come to the light, to the end. Yes, God says, this is all I ask of you, and you will be my disciple. "I wanted to vomit." No, even that, even your nausea, surrender it to me, as you can. It will not be glorious, but you will already know what mercy is, and you will know who I am and who you truly are.

An Advocate

"We have an advocate with the Father, Jesus Christ the righteous" (1 Jn 2:1). "If your heart condemns you, God is greater than your heart" (1 Jn 3:20).

Let us return here to the testimony of Robert Badinter,
who, interrupting his account of Clairvaux's trial, lets his old
master speak about the profession of the advocate:

> Justice, my little one, is not your affair. You do not render
> justice, you decide nothing, you condemn no one, you can-
> not even acquit anyone. Your problem is not to know what is
> or is not just; your only problem, your *raison d'être*, advocate,
> is to defend. You understand, my little one, it is simple. Don't
> say "I do what I do for the sake of justice." That is sometimes
> true, sometimes false, but in any case, it is not important.
> What counts is that you do everything to defend. . . . The
> defense, my little one, is a totality; I mean that you must
> commit yourself totally.[2]

*

For Thérèse, Jesus did not pardon abstractly. The only one
who can pardon the torturer is the one who has been tortured. Only the one who was the object of hatred and the
victim of his thirst for destruction can manifest the impotence of hatred by pardoning the one who hates him, hoping
that this act will be creative of a new history for the one who
was under the hold of hatred. The pardon given by Jesus at
the moment of his death, "Father, pardon them", was a pardon that was weighted with the whole of his history. He had
been pursued, calumniated, jeered at, scorned, ridiculed,
condemned, and was dying as a criminal and a blasphemer. In
pardoning, Jesus hopes that the logic of death of which he
was the victim will not have the last word. His pardon opens
the possibility of a future, and this future is already inscribed
in the reality of his Resurrection. God makes his pardon his
own.

[2] *L'Exécution* (Paris: Grasset, 1973), pp. 42–44.

Jesus opens the future for the sinner himself since he testifies through his pardon that nothing is definitively imprisoned in hatred and that his God is the very One who abolished all the barriers by pardoning those who killed his representative. In this act, pardon is gained for all mankind since the One who pronounced it is ever living. God can no longer be conscripted in order to support the hatreds of clans, races, classes. He can no longer even be conscripted as a guarantor of an implacable justice. God can be invoked only where pardon creates a newness of relations, those that Thérèse exalted throughout her life. By freeing us from hatred through his pardon, Jesus definitively frees the oppressive image of the absolute.

CHAPTER TWELVE

The Return of Satan

"To Bernanos, who asked him in 1945 what the major event of our times was, Malraux replied: 'The return of Satan'— Bernanos, who said that to be Christian is not only to believe in God, which is easy, but to believe in the devil." [1]

On August 16, 1897, in the depths of her sufferings (three days later, Thérèse would receive her last Holy Communion, for she would no longer be able to assimilate even a piece of the Host), Thérèse confided to her sister Céline:

> The devil is around me; I don't see him but I feel him. He is tormenting me; he is holding me with an iron hand to prevent me from taking the slightest relief; he is increasing my pains in order to make me despair. And I can no longer pray! I can only look at the Blessed Virgin and say: "Jesus!". . . *I'm suffering for you*, and the devil doesn't want it! (LC 224)

What does it mean not to believe in the devil? Nothing except to refuse finally to choose mercy. . .

In rediscovering the gaze of the God of Jesus, Thérèse became a missionary to the entire world. She freed us from the worst of all illnesses. By breaking down all fatalism, she brought the ultimate help in the face of evil. That can be expressed in three words: "All are called." If there is evil,

[1] Jean Lacouture, *André Malraux* (Paris: Seuil, 1973), p. 416.

there is never for her, before God, an evil that could exist apart from mercy. Good and evil are not parallel: as if evil could finally be beyond the power of God.

The sickness called Manicheism—wherever it comes from, beginning with certain tendencies within Christianity itself— is present everywhere in our civilization, not only in the consequences of Marxism but also in the very midst of the Church. Everything is an excuse for it. One must "debate" so many things at the risk of letting people believe that evil could remain outside the reach of love and of the omnipotence of God, and thus one must, one day, manage to "eliminate the wicked". The life of Thérèse cries out the opposite: "All are called." Everyone is invited, right now, to accept himself as he is because Christ loves him. A new type of fraternity is born in the gaze of Christ. True rehabilitation, that of mercy, can take place, even for those who think themselves misunderstood, on the margins of society or of the Church, even for those who think themselves far off, even for the good thief. God has put an end to evil, but not as we are tempted to do it: by hiding it or by attributing it to another person or other people. If God takes away evil, he first of all displays it prominently, but he carries what he denounces, and he takes away what he carries. He finally takes care of abolishing it. He breaks the chain of interminable expiations. Mercy is what effects a concentration of evil but what, having effected it, has the faculty of removing this evil and of not letting it spread anew.

The Last Photos of Thérèse

We might be surprised to find a Carmelite designated "patroness of the missions". Of course Thérèse "did" a lot by informing herself, by opening her mind, from Saigon to

Hanoi, by adopting her missionary brothers, by offering her acts of heroism for the salvation of those farthest away, and so on. Yet it is not primarily for all that that she remains "patroness of the missions". It is simpler, stronger. She understood that love situated her in the very place of the Church's birth: the heart of Christ; at the eternal source of all missions: that agony in the life of Christ, in his Passion, of a people to be saved and who refuse it. Henceforth no one has the right to consider any of his brothers as "marginal" to this agony. We are all, for the same reason, part of the "mission"; for all of us shut our eyes to the agony of Christ.

Once again, through her "inspirations", Thérèse obliges us to overturn our usual way of seeing. She instinctively echoes the most profound intuitions of the New Testament about "mission": when, in Saint John, Christ acknowledges his work, it is always by its origin: "Those that the Father has confided to me are more precious than all", "What my Father has made known to me, I have made known to you." He is first of all "sent from the Father". It is the same for Saint Paul and for the Letter to the Hebrews, where the apostle is defined first of all as an ambassador, which is to say as someone who exists as a function of the one whom he represents and from whom he comes. And we find the same with the choice of the last apostle to replace Judas: he had to be taken from among those who had "lived with Christ" and had been "witness to the Resurrection". This is indeed the same intuition to which Thérèse constantly returns in order to legitimate her apostolic role. Once again it is in a letter to Céline that she perhaps expresses this best.

> It was one day when I was thinking of what I could do to save souls, a word of the gospel gave me a real light. In days gone by, Jesus said to His disciples when showing them the fields of ripe corn: "Lift up your eyes and see how the fields

THE RETURN OF SATAN

are already white enough to be harvested," and a little later:
"In truth, the harvest is abundant but the number of laborers
is small, ask then the master of the harvest to send laborers."
What a mystery! . . . Is not Jesus all-powerful? Are not creatures His who made them? Why, then, does Jesus say: "Ask
the Lord of the harvest that he send some workers"? Why?
. . . Ah! it is because Jesus has so incomprehensible a love for
us that He wills that we have a share with Him in the salvation of souls. He wills to do nothing without us. The Creator
of the universe awaits the prayer of a poor little soul to save
other souls redeemed like it at the price of all His Blood. Our
own vocation is not to go out to harvest the fields of ripe
corn. Jesus does not say to us: "*Lower* your eyes, look at the
fields and go harvest them." Our mission is still more sublime.
These are the words of our Jesus: "*Lift* your eyes and see." See
how in my heaven there are empty places; it is up to you to
fill them, you are my Moses praying on the mountain, ask me
for workers and I shall send them, I await only a prayer, a sigh
from your heart!" (LT 135, GC 2:753)

We could continue Thérèse's image with some humor: Do
not lower your eyes in order feverishly to pick up all the
news . . . but "lift your eyes to the work of Christ." For
Thérèse, the "apostolate", that of prayer, of her life, did not
consist in scrutinizing the needs of men—others have that
responsibility—in devouring the news, and so on. Rather, it
consisted in entering into the needs of God, the need of God
to spread life and love on earth, to choose children there to
occupy "the empty places" of his kingdom. This reversal can
be annoying. Is it not the only one that is evangelical, and is
it not the only one that permits us to designate as patroness of
the missions someone who is "useless"?

From 1889 to the last weeks of 1897, it is impossible to
escape the radical theocentrism of Thérèse's apostolic zeal.
She received her brothers from Christ, just as Christ received

them from his Father, and this is why, first of all, "they are more precious than anything", beginning with Pranzini.

Thérèse understood that God is the only one before whom we have the certitude of knowing ourselves to be fully recognized, accepted, loved. The only one who can meet us at the heart of that solitude where we inexorably find ourselves sometimes. The unique One who we know with certainty shares totally the anguish of living and of dying, the one who, one day or another, embraces all men. In the Garden of Olives, in Jesus of Nazareth, God experienced this ordeal more radically than any creature will ever experience it. So, beneath the gaze and in the heart of God, we know that we can be ourselves, without makeup or airs, pride or anger, for our sin itself was crucified with him. What no one in the world could ever achieve, what no political, sociological, or psychological force whatever could do, the mercy of God did: it permitted each one to be himself, freely, like a child, without feeling judged, but, on the contrary, knowing himself to be totally accepted with all his grandeur and misery, nobility and cowardice, self-forgetfulness and withdrawal into himself—it freed each one from all fear. This is how God loves: he meets us there where no human being can meet us.

On June 7, 1897, two days before the certitude of her death seemed clear to her, Thérèse, kneeling, exhausted from illness, posed for a photography session in the Lisieux cloister. These would be the last photos. A twenty-four-year-old face that looks fifty, one of the most moving things that can help us perceive what the Garden of Olives was. One year earlier, the same pose: Thérèse held a lily. Good. Here she holds— one would even say she offers one last time—two images: the Child Jesus and the Holy Face.

THE RETURN OF SATAN

Here we are at the center of the revolutionary intuition of Thérèse of Lisieux after three centuries of Jansenism in the Church.

> He was SILENT before His judges! . . . He made Himself poor that we might be able to give Him love. He holds out His hand to us like a *beggar* so that on the radiant day of judgment when He will appear in His glory, He may have us hear those sweet words: "Come, blessed of my Father, for I was hungry and you gave me to eat. . . ." It is Jesus Himself who spoke these words; it is He who wants our love, who *begs* for it. . . . He places Himself, so to speak, at our mercy, He does not want to take anything unless we give it to Him, and the smallest thing is precious in His divine eyes. (LT 145, GC 2:808)

God is disarmed forever. Since Calvary, every Gospel, every Mass repeats it. God relies on us for the image of himself. God has taken the tenderness of love to the point of letting us shape his face. That is the "folly" of the Incarnation. At the end of history, while we will have to thank God for everything ourselves, in a paradoxical situation, it is God himself who will be able to thank us. That is the secret of Thérèse's joy and her intuition of "heaven": God in response to her love will share his omnipotence with her: "I was hungry. . . . You gave me. . . . What do you want?" "Now, my turn" (LT 157, GC 2:841)!

"I can't fear a God who made Himself so small for me . . . I love Him! For He is only love and mercy!" (LT 266, CG 2:1181).[2] Only Jesus, and Jesus Christ crucified, the Holy Face lifted to the center of the world, could prepare for this: God, "grieved . . . to his heart" (Gen 6:6) by human misery (Ex 3:7) and apparently impotent, a God whose face is like

---

[2] This text, although calligraphed, is by Thérèse. It is her spiritual testament to Abbé Bellière, and it is her last letter; cf. LT 162, GC 2:852.

nothing else, because he is God. Origen, at the beginnings of Christianity, cried out: "It is dangerous to speak of God", of this God, for he is "easily moved". This face is the only one that is absolutely different from all that creatures can tell us: it is that of the folly of the Cross, the one that Thérèse discovered very early.

*

The God of Jesus, the God of Thérèse in everyday life, says only: "Will you?" Defenseless and disarming: "Will you?"

Will you rely, like the prodigal son, on another image of yourself in order to take hope again? Will you, like Zechariah and Magdalen, look beyond your culpability? Will you, with each of the beatitudes, welcome the poor, suffer for justice, peace, mercy? Will you not be afraid of crying? Will you entrust your past and your future? Will you? Finally, will you with me? Will you live your life with me, the true life, the one of hope, of gift, of truth, of joy? It is no longer we alone who purify our ideas or invent our idols; it is no longer we who search for God through courage or concepts: it is God, God himself, who, with the face of Jesus, poses this single question to our search and to us.

PART THREE

HER MESSAGE

CHAPTER THIRTEEN

Daystars

"Advance, advance; rejoice in death which will give you not what you hope for but a night still more profound, the night of nothingness." Whose words are these that we have just quoted, so strong are they? From a rebellious philosopher? From a despairing character out of today's theatre? From a drug addict on the verge of suicide?

It was Thérèse of Lisieux who wrote them, in her bed, on June 9, 1897; three months before she died. She added: "I don't want to write any longer about it; I fear I might blaspheme; I fear even that I have already said too much" (SS 213).

Along with charity and her attention to the greatness of the everyday, along with the absolute intuition of the reciprocity of love with respect to God, there is in the message of Thérèse of Lisieux another response. It was for her the fruit of a battle in the face of death and to the point of death. She insisted that one speak of it as a "message". It was the finest fruit of charity. It was the very offering that Christ made in the face of man's abandonment when, his Holy Face turned toward the center of the world, he cried out: "My God, my God, why have you abandoned me?" We have the same question, the same message, the same gift with Saint Thérèse: that of hope against all hope, or, as she says, her little way of confidence.

The words might well deceive us here: "little way", "little soul", "littleness". With such expressions, one could quickly be tricked into imagining that this is a matter of something easy, while what is actually at stake is probably one of the fundamental decisions orienting the whole of one's life.

It is invaluable to have a witness to show the nuances and the maturity of Thérèse at the time she was proposing her "little way". Sister Marie of the Trinity, at the time of the first process in preparation for beatification, affords some useful information, even if the wording used and transcribed by the Sister, although very close to Thérèse, is perhaps a bit stiff at certain points and needs to be completed by the whole ensemble of Thérèse's other explanations. Here, then, is the first part of the deposition of Sister Marie of the Trinity:

> One day I told her I was going to explain her "little way of love" to my family and friends and have them make the "Act of Oblation" so that they would go straight to heaven. "Oh!" she said, "in that case, be very careful! For our 'little way' could be mistaken for quietism or illuminism if it is badly explained or poorly understood." These words, which were unknown to me, surprised me, and I asked her their meaning. She told me then about a certain Mme. Guyon, who had strayed onto a wrong path. "People must not think that following our 'little way' is following a path of rest and peace, full of sweetness and consolation. Ah! It is quite the opposite!" (PO 456)

What is at issue in Thérèse's "little" way is the ultimate acceptance of life. Neither easy nor difficult. It is not difficult: it is within everyone's reach, and at the very moment when existence seems more miserable than we believed. It is not easy; it is staggering: to trust to the end of the night, which includes everything.

From the Bottom of the Well

> There are always stars in the sky, but we do not always see
> them, for the light of the sun eclipses them. It is only in deep
> and still wells that we can see the stars of the day, which have
> a beauty even more brilliant than those of the night, says a
> legend. Perched high in the sky and inaccessible to our gaze,
> these stars are reflected only in the depths of the earth, on the
> dark mirror of the water that they illumine with their rays.
> And if we do not see them when we look from up above at
> the rim of the well, it is either because the water is not dark
> enough or because the surface of the water is not still enough,
> or because the well is not deep enough. Perhaps even because
> we must not look from outside at the depth of the well but
> from the depth of the well itself.[1]

The meaning of this parable is obvious. Our hearts, cut
one day by grief, our lives plunged at times into darkness and
shadow, can be and are in modern-day humanity, right where
we are, those wells in which this daystar is reflected and in
which it lives, the most beautiful of all, which is named hope.
This star is invisible to the ordinary gaze; it is without apparent existence; but it can become visible to the heart of our
life. It is in the depth of distress, of failure, of anguish, that the
star of Thérèse shines.

*

Picturing the Christian life as a journey, a pilgrimage, an
exodus is classical. Saint Paul defines the Christian by *épectase*,
which is to say, as a "being turned toward what is ahead".
This was repeated or expressed in one way or another by all

---

[1] Olga Bergholtz, *Les Étoiles du jour* (Paris: Plon, 1963), pp. 117, 126.

the spiritual masters. Gregory of Nyssa was one of the first to express it in his commentary on the Exodus, where he imagines the life of the Christian using the image of the Exodus of the people of God. Dionysius the Areopagite, Saint Benedict, William of Saint-Thierry tried to fix the stages or degrees of this journey. Saint Bernard traced the stages of a "ladder of freedom", Teresa of Avila wrote a *Way of Perfection* and the *Interior Castle*, and John of the Cross *The Ascent of Mount Carmel*. The life of the Christian is journey, passage, dynamism.

Several new things appeared in Thérèse's message.

1. She did not speak of "degrees of perfection" as the spiritual masters did; she did not establish her way as an "itinerary" that has stages. Faced with details expressed as intellectual theories by these masters, she experienced her inability to follow these "stages". Her intuition did indeed start from experience. One might say, by way of simplifying, that, faced with the last stage, Thérèse was tempted to think: "I'm not far from it"; but, faced with the first, she observed: "I'll never get there." It was the impossibility of getting to the first stage that opened the way for her. She used quite straightforwardly a still simpler and more current synonym of the word "way", that of "road", when she spoke of surrender as "the road that leads to this Divine Furnace" (SS 188), that is, love, which is the only science she desired (ibid.).

2. This way takes into account the most unavoidable, the most present realities and, one might say, places through which the lives of all men must pass as well as the point of departure for all lives: desire; and the place of difficulty: despair.

She was indeed destined to share both of these fully:

Desire: In the beginning, everything was object, was

marked by her desire, up to the point of anxiety. She was nearly obliged to inflate desire, partly because of the family atmosphere. Being the last, it was a question of doing as well as her sisters. The exemplary value of hope in Saint Thérèse and the essence of the "little way" cannot be understood if one dodges this role of desire: it was present at the beginning, and it would remain despite all failures (see SS 27, 72, 79, 175-76, 193–97, 215, and so on).

Despair. One need only recall Thérèse's way of the cross: the death of her mother; the departure for Carmel of the one who had replaced her mother; the battle with herself, over-whelmed for three years, to the point of neurosis, until she was thirteen and the Christmas conversion; the struggle to enter Carmel; and, from the time of her entrance on, the tragedy of her father's illness, which began three months afterward, to the point of madness. Nine years of Carmel torn by the suffering of her father; the ultimate test of the last eighteen months: the trial of faith in a battle against despair in the face of temptation to doubt about the future, about heaven, about God; and ending with six months of agony and suffocation to the point of being tempted to commit suicide. The last day, her sister, Mother Agnès, would rush to kneel before the Sacred Heart, imploring that Thérèse, abso-lutely at the limit of her strength, would not fall into final despair.

CHAPTER FOURTEEN

The Orphan Girl from Bérésina

With justification, a disproportion has been noted, with respect to Thérèse of Lisieux, between the "little" of what she
did, the "nothing" of her life, and then the "all" of her glory.
A disproportion between the banality of her existence and
the consideration given her, her renown, her success, this
phenomenon of stardom. Although for many others, it is
understandable. When John Paul II beatified Edith Stein, he
beatified a Carmelite who died having been deported, a Jew
who entered the Cologne Carmel, who had been a disciple
of Husserl, one of the great philosophers of that century. She
herself was a philosopher and would be a martyr. And, too,
we can understand that someone like Teresa of Avila, who
founded monasteries and restored an order, or Anne-Marie
Javouhey, who, in the middle of the nineteenth century, trav-
eled the entire world in an attempt to free the slaves, or
Catherine of Siena, who shook the conscience of popes, or
Joan of Arc, who saved France, might be beatified or canonized. But Thérèse? Hers was the banality of a little girl's life,
all enclosed, the life of an adolescent who simply spent a little
time in a Carmel. What is there to interest us in her? To the
point of sending her relics around the world? It this some
kind of ecclesiastical nostalgia in a time of crisis?

A Russian Orthodox philosopher was recently asked what

five people were situated between him and Christ. He re-
plied: Saint Paul, Saint Augustine, Francis of Assisi, Joan of
Arc, and Thérèse of Lisieux. My litany is the same. I would
perhaps simply add a giant of thought: Saint Thomas
Aquinas, and a poor man in accordance with the heart of
God: the Curé of Ars.

Thérèse, a Genius?

In France, only Pascal is perhaps comparable. During my stay
in a German religious house in 1949, my brothers in religion
repeatedly said to me: "We are not capable of inventing beings
like Pascal, Antoine de Saint-Exupéry, or Thérèse of Lisieux."
It is good to go back to the intuitions of Jean Guitton:

1. Most saints preferred heaven to earth. For Thérèse, it
was the opposite. This was an original feature in her that is
more timely than ever: giving full value to the concrete, to
earth, to time, to little things, but with gentleness and in the
name of love. In a certain way, through the importance given
to time and to the present moment, she reversed the relationship between heaven and earth and became one of the rare
mystics who gave priority to earth. She insisted on the value
of the temporal, on the value of the present. She loved this
present moment as if she were already in heaven, because it
was the sole means of offering her freedom. We have already
said that Thérèse made "Norman" use of grace, close to the
manner of the Curé of Ars, with his peasant realism. Time, as
Thérèse knew, is very long. But she also knew that it is very
short, too short: "a true illusion", as Jean Guitton said.

2. We can isolate a second feature of her originality: it is
the sense of the true at first sight. Beyond suspicions, hesita-
tions, interpretations, she had an astonishingly sound and
quick discernment.

3. Another characteristic of her holiness was her ability to do without effort what requires much effort. It is difficult to make an effort. It is still more difficult to make an effort effortlessly. It is perhaps a supreme gift of grace.

4. This same grace led her to discover the foundation of all spiritual life: surrender. Above action, there is something that is the action of action, where life is no longer agitated because it is trust and surrender.

5. From that comes her understanding of love. In its own nature, to love is to put one's trust, but it is also to "lift one's little foot" in order to move farther ahead. What does it mean to love? To love truly? Thérèse had a genius for simplicity that is more useful than ever, after Vatican II, in the midst of the crises that the Church is going through, for example, that of an overly critical rationalism, of theologies that are at times suffocating and suffocated by an itch for interpretations, of fluctuating "hermeneutics". The strength of Islam and of Protestantism is a certain simplicity; now Thérèse leads us back to the Gospel, as John Paul II recalled. Thérèse leads us to the essence, which is the fatherhood of God. We are children. It is a matter of giving proof of it and of living it.

6. A fortunate consequence follows from this understanding. At the threshold of the atomic era, Thérèse helped the Church free herself from maladies that had not been completely cured, those of Jansenism and of Manicheism.

7. We could add her charm, her grace, her poetical gifts, without forgetting her astonishing theological acuity. This intelligent accuracy perhaps explains in part why her story and her autobiography spread so quickly all over the world.

We have said that Thérèse is one of the strongest expressions, in the history of mankind, in the face of two "abysses" (she often used this word): that of freedom and the desire to fulfill her potential and that of an interlocutor named God. Now, in order to go all the way, she reopened the door of hope and gave back to the helpless the true face of God throughout an existence that was more eventful than one might think. That began very early. She was sent away to be nursed because of the cancer of her mother, who could not nurse her. Events rushed on. We mentioned them above: the death of her mother, the departure for Carmel of the one who had replaced her mother. That would be repeated at the age of thirteen with the departure of her other sister, Marie, for Carmel. That would be the third death of her mother. Thérèse's nerves were not going to hold up. Joan of Arc would hold up. Between her thirteenth and seventeenth year we witness Joan's impressive silence. Thérèse, however, would not. Once her sister Pauline entered Carmel, she had a right to only one or two minutes at the end of the half-hour visit in the parlor. She would admit later: "Ah, what I could suffer in that parlor of Carmel." She would speak again in terms of very hard, unbearable suffering of the time when her father was buried. She said nothing at the time. Nor were there any complaints, but this was the depth of distress.

Thérèse had staked everything on trust in a mother. Now she was going to be, during her life, obliged to solitude. At ten years, she had fallen sick, much more profoundly than they thought, to the point of death. It was not merely a matter of a little girl's caprices; there were continual headaches, pains in her side, her heart; she was covered with a rash; she lost her appetite; her personality was upset; she no longer slept; she became excessively weepy. One day she unfortunately called her aunt "mama"; her cousin reacted quickly by saying: "My mama is not your mama; you don't have one any more." Her uncle then recalled the memory of his sister, Thérèse's mother. She collapsed in tears; seized by trembling, she was very upset. Doctors were vague but very pessimistic. They wrote: "Very serious illness with which no child has ever been afflicted." Her father, who was in Paris at the time, was recalled and, encountering the shattered face of the cook, believed Thérèse to be dead. The illness persisted: there were crises with frightening hallucinations; they were dismayed; and this went on for months. There was a temporary recovery the day she saw her sister once again at Pauline's clothing day in Carmel. Then there was a relapse that was more serious still. Thérèse was lucid. Totally lucid. She herself specifies: "I appeared to be almost always delirious, saying things that had no meaning. And still I am *sure* that I *was not deprived of the use of my reason for one single instant*" (SS 62). For the doctor, this was not hysteria. Her father wondered if his daughter, who seemed to be going crazy, was not going to die.

They were praying in the Carmel. It was a Novena to Our Lady of Victories. A statue of the Virgin had been put in her room. On Pentecost, there was the "grace of the smile". During the novena, Thérèse never stopped calling as usual "Mama, Mama . . .", while moaning and delirious. She would recount later:

> Finding no help on earth, poor little Thérèse had also turned towards the Mother of heaven, and prayed with all her heart that she take pity on her. All of a sudden the Blessed Virgin appeared *beautiful* to me, so *beautiful* that never had I seen anything so attractive; her face was suffused with an ineffable benevolence and tenderness, but what penetrated to the very depths of my soul was the "*ravishing smile of the Blessed Virgin*." (SS 65–66)

And Thérèse promised not to speak of it. That would be a new crisis for her, for her sisters would notice there had been a change. Her older sister [Marie] was insistent and forced the secret from her soul. Thérèse recounted the reason for her cure, but she had a relapse, for she had the impression of having betrayed something, an impression that would remain for five years. Her guilt increased. There was her First Communion, but the scruples began again. Then there was the journey of her father to Constantinople, then Marie's entrance into Carmel, which she felt as a new death of her mother.

It is surprising that it took researchers and historians so long to discover Thérèse's motherly role and understanding. It is enough to look at her life to see how important this was. But everything comes to pass eventually. In his long study, *L'Orpheline de la Bérésina: Thérèse de Lisieux. Essai de psychanalyse socio-historique*, the director of research at the CNRS, Jacques Maître, notes:

> Thérèse of Lisieux seems to me a very great virtuoso in mystical creativity. After her, God has never been the same. While the God of her acquaintances was a terrifying God, who demanded penitence and punishment, Thérèse had the idea of a God suitable for infants, purely good, of whom one had nothing to fear. One can easily see that there has been a rupture between that bogeyman and this good mother who would never take faults into consideration and who gives love if we ask for it the least bit. The change introduced by Thérèse has in the end proved lasting. Today, for example, we could not imagine in France the bishops declaring that the existence of AIDS is a divine punishment. It is probable that a good portion of French Catholics think that, but those in authority cannot say it. That is one of the consequences of the break where Thérèse's name is significantly inscribed. A century ago, people saw God's whip behind all catastrophes.

The journal *Le Monde* itself devoted a one-page article to this book.[1] It took a century for the "researchers" to discover a

---

[1] "L'Itinéraire de Jacques Maître", *Le Monde*, December 16, 1995.

message that, with no need for psychoanalysis, sociology, or approximations ("God's whip"!), the poor of the earth, with their instinct of faith, had been able to discern a hundred years ago—a message written by Thérèse with her blood, following Isaiah and the gospel.

Her Race of Giants

At fourteen years, there was her conversion, the turnaround at Christmas 1886. Thérèse entered more into prayer on the occasion of the Pranzini affair. She was answered. Then it was the struggle to enter Carmel. She had to convince her father, meet with the refusal of the superior, that of the bishop, the resistance of her uncle. Then it was the departure for Rome. Thérèse decided, if the occasion presented itself, to go ask authorization to enter Carmel from the pope himself. She herself recounted her visit in Paris, which had impressed her: the puppet show in the Tuileries, the Louvre, the Bastille, the shops of the Printemps, the Palais-Royal, Sacré-Coeur, the Arc de Triomphe. It would not be, as was long thought, the elevators in the Printemps that would furnish her with the marvelous image of the mercy of God, but those in the hotel where she stayed in Rome. Instead of being determined to climb the stairs step to step, she knew that there was a divine elevator and that someone had taken her in his arms. In Paris, her family had stopped at a hotel near Our Lady of Victories, the Boulois hotel, not far from the church, a hotel we can no longer visit, since it has been destroyed.

On November 4, during Mass, at the feet of Our Lady of Victories, Thérèse was freed after four years of distress. She writes: "It was truly she who had smiled at me and cured me."

All that might pass for the tales of a spoiled little girl. Yet the experience of solitude and of fragility borne to the end by Thérèse was not over. There was a happy year. There were two of them in her life, we must repeat: 1887, the one that would follow the pilgrimage of Our Lady of Victories; then 1895, in Carmel, the year of the Act of Oblation to Merciful Love. And that was all.

Very quickly, in Carmel, she discovered that she was "good for nothing", and she was made to understand this. She would have liked to have the office of laundry or the infirmary, but she was not given anything.

Then the tragedy of her father occurred. After running away and an operation for a cyst behind his ear that had created a patch of suffering as big as the palm of one's hand, he was escorted to the psychiatric hospital in Caen. The hospital reports about M. Martin are still available. We know about his lucidity, his humility, his kind-heartedness. Thérèse, too, knew what was said in Lisieux and even in Carmel. If her father, whom she loved madly, had been committed, it was perhaps her fault. If only she had not entered religion. Having become paralyzed after three years in the hospital, he was released. He would die several months later. There would be only a single visit from her father to the Carmel during those five years. He was in a wheelchair that would be used again for Thérèse when she herself was sick. During that last meeting, there was only a single look, but not a word; M. Martin pointed to heaven; that was all.

Trial of Faith

And there were the last eighteen months of struggle in her "race of giants". The impression that everything had been pointless, that there was nothing more after death except nothingness. This is what has been called her "trial of faith" or what she herself would call the "night of nothingness". Just after the first hemoptysis of Good Friday 1896, all joy in living abruptly disappeared. An unexpected suffering came crashing down on Thérèse. During this Easter season, she entered into the most opaque interior darkness, which lasted for eighteen months. Here she who had been thinking of going very quickly to heaven was left without any sense of faith. She would speak of it to no one except her prioress, Mother Marie de Gonzague, to Abbé Youf, because he was the confessor for the Carmel, and to a preacher passing through, Father Godefroid Madelaine. Abbé Youf would say to her only that one must not think too much about such things, and Father Godefroid would ask her how she managed to look so joyful in front of her Sisters. In fact, Mother Agnès would understand Thérèse's trial only many months later. Her older sister Marie would know nothing about it until after Thérèse's death. The prioress, Mother Marie de Gonzague, sensed that it was serious. She reported it and asked the advice of Father Marie Abric, abbot of the Trappist monastery of Aiguebelle. It is enough to read the poetry written by Thérèse at this time and the *Story of a Soul* to understand the sharpness and the bewildering nature of what Thérèse lived during all those months. She did not put any states of soul on display, and yet she gave many accurate, precise signs of a tragedy that was at times terrible, with Nietzschean accents.

Rather than a trial of faith, we should speak of a trial of hope. In order to understand this trial, a few remarks are necessary, looking both ahead and back.

Looking ahead, it is not enough to refer to the concern, animated by a certain current apologetic, to remain close to and understanding of our contemporaries who are marked by a certain atheism. That would supposedly have a "purifying" role. There is no need to play around with that. The negation or rejection of God does not of itself have a purifying aim, but rather a negative one.

Still looking ahead, it is not irrelevant to recall that, in any act of faith and in the heart of the believer, God alone can testify to God through a current Pentecost. With all our power, we can never have "evidence" of faith; that would be a Last Judgment; but "certitude" is something else. One believes that one believes. The reply of Joan of Arc to her judges, who were setting a trap for her, expresses that in a well-known phrase. When they asked her if she was in a state of grace, she replied: "If I am not, may God place me there; if I am, may God keep me there." We cannot know if we are in a state of grace. Nor can we leave faith in order to know if we have faith. We trust, or we do not.

Looking back, three remarks can be useful in order to situate Thérèse's trial. First of all, it is absolutely necessary to avoid anything that might risk leading us to think of a perverse God when we speak of the role of trials and temptations in a life. We can hope that soon the translation of the Our Father will finally be revised. It is not a matter of asking God not to "lead us into temptation", which presupposes a certain horror in the idea we have of God, but we can ask him not to let us enter into trials.

Second, it is perhaps good to situate the point of Thérèse's trial elsewhere. Was she not more concerned with hope than with faith? When Christ asked his Father "Why have you abandoned me", he did so only because he knew himself to be in the hand of his Father. Likewise, Thérèse did not first of all doubt that God existed. She asked herself about nothingness. The object of faith is that God is light and that this light is good and thus comprehensible if one recognizes it as good. Hope adds something else to faith. Demons have faith; they do not have hope. The light of God is no longer for them an object of desire; they no longer expect anything from it. For the believer, not only is the light of God a good, but it is *desirable* for him, because it saves him. It is at that point that Thérèse was tried: she had the impression of no longer having such desires. It was her hope that was crucified. Her life followed the same course as the prophets had known, the same one that Saint Thomas Aquinas described so perfectly. At the beginning of his theological career, he said that hope has two objects: first of all happiness, beatitude. And at that moment, this was for him the principal one: as happiness is a difficult thing, one has need of God's help. At that time, this help, this alliance, was but the second object of hope. At the end of his theological career, Thomas Aquinas changed his point of view (it was one of the rare subjects of reflection on which he would modify his doctrine). He then affirmed that what is primary in hope is, first of all, not the desire of beatitude, but the help of God, his alliance with us. There we have the key intuition of the whole mystery of hope that, from Abraham to Thérèse of Lisieux, illumines the path of sanctity. God, indeed, makes a promise to Abraham, that of beatitude and of eternity. He is to have more descendants than the number of stars; and for that, God enters into an alliance with Abraham, saying to him: "I will be with you." The whole of Abraham's life is going to consist in putting the alliance and trust in God above any desire for the promise. This is the same trial that Thérèse experienced. If God offered his help, his alliance, it was because "God cannot promise less than God." Thérèse could no longer keep God within the limits of her consciousness, to the point of experiencing the dizzying thoughts of nothingness and suicide.

We should mention, too, the certitude that Thérèse had in consoling Jesus during this period. She was with Mary at the

foot of the Cross. For someone who suffers, the only consolation is to know that his suffering has served some purpose.
Thérèse, through her trust and her silence, gave witness to
her Jesus that his Passion had served some purpose and that
she herself was willing to accomplish in her heart and in her
body what was lacking in the Passion of Christ. She was, with
Mary, co-redemptrix, associated with the salvation of the
world.

*

On June 9, 1897, she was told that she would not last the
night. On August 19, she could no longer even receive
Communion, not even a little particle of the Host. And she
died on September 30. She died from pulmonary tuberculosis, which led to a type of suffering of which we scarcely
have any idea today thanks to streptomycin, which has been
used for the past fifty years. The lungs wasted away. One
died of thirst and suffocation, to say nothing of the "bar-
baric" treatments, as Professor Marrou said, in thinking of
vesication, or blistering, of ignipuncture, and so on, treatments to which we will return later on. Reports of the most
surprising measures taken in an attempt to relieve Thérèse
are preserved in the archives of the Carmel's infirmary. The
evening before her death, Mother Agnès, who had been her
prioress, would go and throw herself at the foot of the statue
of the Sacred Heart and beg Christ not to let her sister
Thérèse die blaspheming.

Thérèse would pass away while saying "Jesus, Jesus! I love
you." She was twenty-four years old.

*

We have already brought up certain objections or pseudo-objections that could be made about Thérèse of Lisieux. It is obvious that they will arise again and will always be present in each generation: a language different from our own, the apparent banality of her poetry; we would have to admit that, with Thérèse, under the appearance of verse à la Lamartine, we are dealing with poetry in its "primitive" state; her conception of the world, of suffering, of life in community and her cloistered life. After fifty years of careful examination, I repeat: These objections are the result of ignorance. They are subtle, tenacious, but false. It is necessary to go and see.

Thérèse did not allow herself to weaken. "When I feel nothing and am incapable of praying," she writes, "I have had the experience of practicing virtue; it is then the time to seek little occasions, little nothings that give more pleasure to Jesus than the dominion of the world or even than martyrdom suffered generously."

Thérèse knew very quickly that nothing could be done on the path of true life without a battle. She was not afraid that truth would diminish her. The truth without Jesus was too hard. Jesus without truth was an illusion. We see this in the book that was on Bernanos' bedstand, and on that of Mounier, that of Marc Sangnier, and of so many others: the *Novissima Verba*, or *Last Conversations*. The struggle in the face of sickness and death had in reality begun a year earlier, with the first spitting of blood the night before Good Friday. That night, after the hemoptysis, she wondered what was happening; she did not relight her lamp; for a year she did not speak of it to her two sisters. "On Good Friday, however, Jesus wished to give me the hope of going to see Him soon in heaven. . . . I felt something like a bubbling stream mounting to my lips. I didn't know what it was, but I thought that perhaps I was going to die and my soul was flooded with joy"

(SS 210). The shock was such that several days later she entered into the night. Nothing more of the realities of faith, the absence of all consolation. When her prioress asked her to write a poem or something more for the *Story of a Soul*, because Mother Marie de Gonzague thought that it was easy for her to sing what she believed, Thérèse replied "I do not sing what I believe but what I 'want' to believe."

Of the twelve priests whom she had encountered during her life, only two, for the space of a confession, had truly helped her.

Two days before she was "sure of dying soon", according to her expression, her sister Céline had made her pose three times, on her knees in the center of the cloister, in order to take the last photographs. It was Monday, June 7, the day after Pentecost. She appears in them to be tense with all her courage, her face lined and her hands clinging to two images that she holds close: the Holy Face and the Child Jesus. When death came closer, they would bring, to a room adjoining the infirmary, a blessed candle, candlesticks, a holy water basin, and sprinkler for the preparation of her burial. She suspected this and asked that the objects be placed so that she might see them. Her sister Céline, in her *Conseils et souvenirs* (perhaps one of the most beautiful books of spirituality there is), recounts the episode: "Thérèse looked at them from time to time with a complacent air and said, smiling: 'You see that candle there, when the Thief carries me away, they will put that in my hand, but they shouldn't give me the candlestick, it's too ugly!" And Céline adds that "Thérèse inspected all the details of her burial and talked about it in terms that made us smile when we would rather have cried."

While maintaining this incredible strength of truth, Thérèse would admit twice that she had been tempted by suicide (cf. LC September 22, no. 6, pp. 258, 295). She would insist that they not leave medications too close to the patients. She said: "Ah! If I didn't have faith, I would never be able to endure so much suffering, I am surprised there aren't more atheists who take their own lives."

Nothing could thwart her humor. "Life is sad", she is told. Then she replies: "It is only to the things of heaven, to what must never die, that we must give this real name [life]; and, under this title, life is not sad, but happy, very happy!" (LC 265). She learned to lean on someone else. And she wanted to cry out her secret when she wrote:

> As far as little ones are concerned, they will be judged with great gentleness. And one can remain little, even in the most formidable offices, even when living for a long time. If I were to die at the age of eighty, if I were in China, anywhere, I would still die, I feel, as little as I am today. And it is written: "At the end, the Lord will rise up to save the gentle and the humble of the earth." It doesn't say "to judge", but "to save".

We must truly return to the cries of the great rebels whom we have already mentioned in order to understand just how far the cry of Thérèse goes.

CHAPTER FIFTEEN

The Course of Hope

Everything was set to make Thérèse withdraw into herself.
Everything in her life should have led her to distress, weari-
ness, rebellion, or despair. And it was just the opposite; she
untiringly reinvented the path of hope. We can mark it out in
seven stages, even if she herself did not construct a theory of
these different moments. They are clear. Father Conrad De
Meester has analyzed them remarkably well in his two books
Dynamique de la confiance and *Les Mains vides.*[1]

1. Thérèse's path begins in a simple way. She starts with a
twofold observation, one with which we are all familiar.
Within her dwells a desire that she discovers to be both very
great and deep-rooted. Very early on, we could say from the
age of four years, if not even from the age of two, she discovered this immense desire to love. She gives us some information about this on November 1, 1896, in one of her long
letters to Father Roulland: "Our Lord, willing for Himself
alone my first glance, saw fit to ask [for] my heart in the
cradle, if I can so express myself" (L 201, GC 2:1016).

2. But she is clear-sighted enough to see very quickly that
she will not even manage to get up the first step of this
stairway she must climb in order to be someone "good", as

---

[1] *Dynamique de la confiance* (Paris: Cerf, 1969) and *Les Mains vides* (Paris: Cerf,
1972).

177

she still thinks God wants her to do. The elevator in a hotel in Rome provides her with the image that allows her to understand that there is another way besides the stairway. The "elevator" is the very mercy of God, who takes her in his arms in order to carry her and raise her up to himself.

3. Yet temptations do not disappear, the same temptations that are the lot of all human beings: either rebellion or aggressiveness. She has the twofold experience of the lack of understanding by others in her regard and of her own discouragement with herself that would lead her to abandon her "dreams". All of that continuing, of course, to be covered over with good intentions: to do as her sisters did, to be someone good, to join those who are trying their hand at the world championship of holiness.

4. Faced with failures and temptations, when she is taken to be "good for nothing" in her Carmel, the desire that dwells in her resists, remains, and holds firm. She concludes that it does not come from her alone. It is not she who has given this image to herself. It comes to her from somewhere else. That means that this idea she is making of herself does not belong to her. She must therefore learn to turn it over to someone else, to the one she loves.

5. Once again, failures, impotence, inability become heavier, more present, and painful, and precisely within the will to do good, within what is legitimately close to her heart, her family and her vocation. There were the failures of her sister Mother Agnès, when the latter was elected prioress; the failures of another sister, Céline, during the first years after she entered the Carmel; the tragedy of her father; her own fears in her role of novice mistress; sleeping at prayer; finally the confusion of the last eighteen months, when she feels as though she is sitting at the "table of the worst materialists". When her prioress speaks to her of

heaven, she replies, "There is nothing more than a wall."
What Paul Valéry would say shortly before dying to his
friend Professor Mondor, Thérèse of Lisieux would say fifty
years earlier, in exactly the same way: "But my Mother, it is
not a veil that separates me from heaven; it is a wall. There
is nothing more." It is a failure. "It seems to me the shadows
are mocking me, saying: You're dreaming."

6. At this moment, she has nothing left on which to depend. Her strength? She has no more left; there is the total
exhaustion of her illness. She has no more desires. With
respect to the esteem of others or the reputation of her
family, the illness of her father as the object of pity has
removed any illusion from her. What else remains for her but
to hold firm and go on? Her little way. Which is to say, her
weakness, her inability itself, her distress, her night, her nothingness itself, in order to reach God and, through trust, to
force the shadows themselves to have a meaning.

7. Then Thérèse enters the last circle of hope. To be
Christian does not mean, first of all, "to be someone good",
which was the noble but dangerous illusion of the Stoics and
the Jansenists. For Thérèse, because of her inability, it is a
question of learning to rely on someone else. Learning to
change her point of support, because then one offers to God
the one thing he cannot achieve without us, the offering of
our freedom. It is not, in the first place, fantasies or even
pious ideas that count, but gestures or small everyday actions.
"The good God shows me the truth", she said about them.
The impossible step is possible. It is trust that makes what we
thought was too far away to be within hand's reach after all.

With one stroke, Thérèse exploded the threats that had
been stifling Christianity for centuries. It was necessary to be
"good" to approach God? Thérèse suggested the opposite.
Offered to all, her little way, from desire to the despair that is

the fate of all men, can become for all, from darkness to trust, the path that finds God. Thérèse showed that what seemed reserved to privileged, distinguished spirits, to the great mystics, is proposed for all.

It is precisely when one is alone and reaching the banks of the Promised Land that fear, temptations, and lassitude—in family life or work as well as in prayer—are Thérèse's treasures on God's path. She worked out before us this acceptance, proposed to everyone, of the night of the spirit, but in gentleness. And here she encountered the most destitute, the most lost, the poorest, those who no longer have any support—just as she met the greatest rebels and the greatest revolutionaries when she set out. "Freedom for us!"

Thérèse did indeed sense the infinite strength that could eventually lead to revolt. But we must immediately add that the only chance to keep this resource is to rely on the one who loves us. And that on one condition: not to seek elsewhere some other strength, whether aesthetical, moral, ideological, satisfying for ourselves because we could maintain our place in history, because we could leave a beautiful image of ourselves, because we could fulfill our itinerary.

Thérèse knew she was not capable of that. She knew that if she was still like that, it was because she had not yet gone the whole way in seeking a true reliance on another.

Thérèse even had to give up the ability to receive Communion. That shattered her beyond the point of tolerance. She wept on August 19, 1897. "Without doubt, it is a great grace to receive the sacraments, but when the good God does not permit it, it is good, all the same. Everything is grace", she said on June 5. Bernanos would base his whole novel *The Diary of a Country Priest* on that sentence of Thérèse: "Everything is grace." That did not stop Thérèse from crying that day, doubting future existence, abandoned by God, whom she could not receive, while others shook their heads around her.

What Thérèse lived, this purification of hope, would this not be the providential image offered to the Church? If Thérèse is still the saint of the twenty-first century, it is when, following Thérèse's example, the Church enters collectively and individually into trial, into questions, fog, shadows, at once painful and marvelous. Would this not be the time of trust? "My folly is to hope", Thérèse said before dying.

CHAPTER SIXTEEN

The Power of Silence

The Flautist of the Orchestra

It was not boring in the Lisieux Carmel. Thérèse was profoundly happy in her family as in her religion. She insisted on it. More than fifty times in the *Story of a Soul* she applies this term "happy" to herself. It is one of the ten most frequently used words in her letters and in the *Last Conversations* (along with "happiness", "joy", and "pleasure").

If, in the orchestra of the Son of God, Philip Neri and Thomas More, princes of humor and of the smile, play the trumpet and the double bass, Thérèse of Lisieux, along with Francis of Assisi, most certainly play the role of flautist or oboist in it: precise, clear, unexpected, never hurting the ear.

It is undoubtedly impossible for anyone who did not lead the religious life before 1950 to imagine to what extent community life of this type, whose customs had varied so little for some three to seven centuries, depending on the religious order, could at one and the same time follow a penitential regime of incredible strictness (the cold, the lack of sleep, the fast) and yet blossom with a fraternal and spontaneous joy. Certainly one would never have laughed with such goodheartedness as in the convents. "Mystic, comic: everything suits her." Let us not forget Thérèse's humor. It could have been cruel with respect to others. It was the opposite. It was unfailingly at her own expense. One day someone should show what she owed to her father in this respect. Their relationship was in part that of two "comics".[1] Thérèse was very gifted when it came to imitations: "She had a particular aptitude for imitating the tone of voice and mannerisms of other people", Léonie would say during the process (PO 347). This humor[2] was not at all secondary. It was with her burst of laughter that Thérèse eluded and will always elude the regime of the "confectioners" who regularly surround her. It is through the extraordinary in the ordinary that a possible holiness is established for all.

To Liberate Holiness

Francis of Assisi would probably have made an odd CEO. The history of his order has demonstrated this well. Everything need not be asked of everyone. Thérèse did not have all qualities. She did indeed have limits. It is here that her humor seems essential. As we have said, it was the form taken in her by both the rigor of the true (but with tenderness) and the understanding of limits (but without any false indulgence) (cf. DE 781–82)—as well as the patience of the little way and the acceptance of no longer being master of herself. Thérèse had chosen the opposite of the "grandeurs" and the spirituality of

[1] M. Martin has been too often described as a patriarchal dreamer. There was a festive atmosphere about Les Buissonnets in which much maturity was hidden under childlike appearances. The word "comic" is the right one for Thérèse, but it might seem exaggerated for M. Martin. And yet, . . . was there not between them a surprising complicity that, under an innocuous appearance, betrayed the same wisdom, the same sense of the relative, of the at times tragic "comic"?

[2] On the humor of Thérèse, cf. SS 54, 57, 139, 223–24, 243–44; DE 781–82; CG 1:395; CG 2:996, note b fin (when she imitates the accent of the Carmel's confessor), etc.

the *grandes dames*, stemming from the misunderstood Bérullism by which the Carmel was marked at that time. She was running counter to that mentality and remained courageously faithful to her intuition, contrary to certain Sisters in the convent.[3] Certainly she kept that taste for effacement and the tenacity of her mother, Zélie Martin, but in Thérèse it became a secret for the whole of her life: she accepted being "nothing", being found "nothing", and knowing herself to have been found so (cf. CSG 20). "And then she, who was attached to faithfulness in small things, the preferred field of the poor man, simple and realistic, she freed sanctity from the prejudice that surrounded her." [4] She did not value apparently extraordinary things, "brilliant actions", as she said; this was not her little way. Yes, she liberated holiness. We have spoken of "democratization". Thomas Merton said: "The 'Little Way' of Therese of Lisieux is an explicit renunciation of all exalted and disincarnate spiritualities that divide man against himself, putting one half in the realm of angels and the other in an earthly hell." [5]

Her Great Weapon Was Silence

"Experience has shown me too late that one cannot explain beings by their vices, but, on the contrary, by what they have

---

[3] For example, Sister Saint-Jean-Baptiste (cf. L 230, GC 2:1100–1101, and n. 2, p. 1102. And Mother Marie de Gonzague? A "*grande dame*", it is true, but more by nature and social rank. On the religious level, there must be no mistake about it: there was a certain simplicity in her; a former pupil of the Visitation monastery at Caen, she had kept a Salesian, not a Jansenist, stamp; cf. LC 162, GC 2:905–6; the tone of this note gives some idea of the atmosphere of the Carmel of Lisieux, which was very close to Teresa of Avila.

[4] C. De Meester, "Actualité de Thérèse de Lisieux", *Carmel* 16:330.

[5] Thomas Merton, *The Way of Chuang Tzu* (New York: New Directions, 1965), p. 12.

kept intact, pure, by what remains in them of childhood, so deep that one must search for it." [6]

Must we go down so deep in order to grasp in what a liberating way Thérèse's virtue was manifested? After the first process for the beatification, in 1910, some wondered if she had suffered enough. Then, at the second process, of 1915–1917, we see the unfortunate Sisters doing their utmost to emphasize the sufferings of Thérèse, the incomprehension of Mother Marie de Gonzague, and so on. For us, Thérèse did still better, and more simply.

It was said of Thomas Aquinas that he was able to become a saint without annoying others. Thérèse's virtue would be annoying if it had the nature of exceptional suffering or a lesson in spirituality. It was a simple, everyday nature, realistic, playful, coarse and at times cruel, but within reach of everyone.

Her sisters were not fooled.

At the beginning of her illness, being obliged to go take some medications a few minutes before meals, one old Sister was surprised by this and complained about it, finding it irregular. Just one word from Sister Thérèse of the Child Jesus would have been enough to excuse herself and restore calm to this Sister. She was very careful not to say anything, taking as her model the conduct of the Holy Virgin, who preferred to let herself be defamed rather than excuse herself to Saint Joseph. She spoke to me often of this conduct. . . . Like Mary, her great weapon was silence . . . , that reserve was her strength and the foundation of her perfection. (Sister Geneviève, CSG 27)

"How many treasures we would win in religious life if we willed to do what Thérèse did: put up with everything without saying anything." [7]

[6] Georges Bernanos, *Lettre aux Anglais* (Paris: Gallimard, 1946), p. 92.

[7] Sister Marie of the Sacred Heart, May 1909, retreat notes; notebook a, p. 40; described in DE 836, no. 8, a.

She herself returned to it constantly and explained it clearly. It is simple, unexpected, as varied as everyday conditions: Learn not to defend or justify yourself, not to judge in haste, to respect secrets, to go to the point of blood to keep silent.

> When we're misunderstood and judged unfavorably, what good does it do to defend or explain ourselves? Let the matter drop and say nothing. It's so much better to say nothing and allow others to judge us as they please! We don't see in the Gospel where Mary explained herself when her sister accused her of remaining at Jesus' feet, doing nothing! She didn't say: "Oh, Martha, if you only knew the joy I am experiencing, if you only heard the words I hear! And besides, it's Jesus who told me to remain here." No, she preferred to remain silent. O blessed silence that gives so much peace to souls!" (LC April 6, 1897, no. 1, p. 36)

> Oh! How few perfect religious there are, who do nothing, or next to nothing, saying: I'm not obliged to do that, after all. There's no great harm in speaking here, in satisfying myself there. How few there are who do everything in the best way possible! And still these are the most happy religious. Take silence for example, what good it does to the soul, what failures in charity it prevents, and so many other troubles of all kinds. I speak especially about silence because it's on this point that we fail the most. (LC August 6, 1897, no. 5, p. 137)

> When one is very sick in body, everyone works to relieve you; if it's a lung problem, they get rid of drafts, the infirmarian is there to see that there's nothing you need. Ah! Why don't we do the same for the spiritual illnesses of our Sisters? That is what the good God asks of me, and, if I get better, I will continue to do it with all my heart. If a Sister is sick spiritually, disagreeable in everything, everyone stays away from her, frowns on her, instead of seeking to relieve her, and it is at her that they sometimes cast hurtful words . . . at her,

who has no strength and is incapable of bearing them! It is rather with those who are healthy that one should act that way, for they, who are going along well, could endure humiliation, lack of consideration, neglect, with good humor. Well, it is for sick souls that I want to reserve my smiles, my affection, and my consideration, that is where I find true charity. (DE April 6, p. 393)

When she was sick, Thérèse would go even farther:

Little sisters, pray for the poor sick who are dying. If you only knew what happens! How little it takes to lose one's patience! You must be kind towards all of them without exception. I would not have believed this formerly. (LC August 3, no. 4, p. 130)

Thérèse said it and demonstrated it.

When she entered Carmel, I must say there was a perceptible trend toward laxity. Several nuns were undoubtedly observant, but there were others, and quite a large number of them, who drifted into abuses. The Servant of God applied herself to her duty without worrying about what the others were doing. I never saw her stop to join the groups that gathered around Mother Prioress to hear the latest news when she came out of the parlor or listen to uncharitable conversations. In our great family difficulties, she was much more courageous than we were. After we had heard painful news in the parlor, such as our father's state of health, rather than seek to comfort herself by talking with us about it; she immediately resumed her community responsibilities. (Testimony of Mother Agnès, PO 150)

If, for instance, someone forgot to serve her in the refectory, she was happy about it and avoided drawing attention to it. She would say, "I am like the real poor; there's no point in making a vow of poverty if it's not to suffer it." Sometimes a

Sister would plagiarize one of her thoughts. She found this quite natural and said that because of her poverty she had no more claim to this kind of property than she had to any other. (Testimony of Mother Agnès, PO 170)

The Servant of God was faithful in keeping any outbursts of passion under control. . . . Although she had a very lively imagination, she never got excited. . . . She advised me never to tell her about something that annoyed me while I was still upset. "When you tell someone, even Mother Prioress, about some argument, never do it to have the Sister who caused it corrected or so that the thing you're complaining about might stop; rather, speak with detachment of heart. When you don't feel that detachment, if there is still even a spark of emotion in your heart, it is more perfect to keep quiet and wait . . . because talking about it often only aggravates it." She always practiced this advice in her personal conduct, and you never saw her run to our Mother in the heat of combat; she always waited until she was in control of herself. (Sister Geneviève of St. Teresa, PO 294)

Her older sister Marie would be nearly astonished by this: "It is not usual to see always the same equanimity of soul, the same smile on the lips . . . even during her greatest trials, to such an extent that I did not know of her sufferings, for instance, in her great temptations against the faith, except through reading her manuscript after her death" (testimony of Sister Marie of the Sacred Heart, PO 244-45).

The Strength to Resist

I was thirteen years old when my father told me he was going to have me learn drawing. We were both there, Thérèse and I, and I saw her eyes burning with envy, and I expected that she would receive the same favor. In fact, my father said:

"And you, my little Queen, would you like to learn drawing?" She was going to answer, but Marie spoke up, saying that the house was already filled with "lousy paintings" that had to be framed, and she won the case. Thérèse didn't answer, and no one guessed what she was feeling, but later, several weeks before her death, recalling this incident, she confided to me that she had felt such a strong desire to complain that she still wondered, after so many years, how she had had the strength to resist it. (Sister Geneviève, NPPO 77; GC 1:210, n. 1)

From the moment she entered Carmel, although she was only fifteen years old, she was treated without any consideration and was served the leftovers that were closest to going bad. In the kitchen they said: "No one would eat that; let's give it to Sister Thérèse of the Child Jesus, who never refuses anything." So we saw the omelette or herring that had been cooked on Sunday reappear on her plate up to the end of the week. In refectory, she had to share with the Sister who sat next to her at table a little bottle of cider that contained scarcely enough for two glasses; well, she never drank any of it, so as not to deprive her neighbor. She could have taken some of the water in the jug, but she abstained so that no one would notice. . . . Three days before her death, when she was tortured by fever, she refrained from asking for some water in which a bit of ice had been put; she also refrained from asking for some grapes, when someone forgot to put them within reach. When I saw her looking at her glass, I perceived her mortification, and I said: "Would you like some iced water?"

"Oh! I would like some very much", she answered me.

"But," I scolded, "our Mother has obliged you to ask for all you need; do so, then, out of obedience."

"I do ask for all I need", she said to me. . . . "If I didn't have grapes, I would not ask for any."

. . . She did not ask for anything back if someone took it. . . . She let the intellectual gifts that God had given her so abundantly be stolen from her, so to speak, for at recreation, if another profited from her retorts, which were so witty and sharp, by repeating them as if they were her own, she willingly gave her the honor of amusing the others, without making known their source. (Testimony of Sister Marie of the Sacred Heart, PO 251–52)

It has been noted that at recreation she never spoke or gave her opinion without being asked, and yet at times, with her lively spirit, what clever, pointed retorts burned on her lips! She had so much of the same discretion in her parlor visits that even among her family Thérèse was said to be a nobody, or rather she passed unnoticed; it was said that, since she "was too young when she entered the convent, her education had been cut short and that she would feel the effects of it her whole life." (Testimony of Sister Geneviève, NPPO 93)

During the last days of her life [it was in the middle of summer], when she was burning with fever, I wanted to remove the sheet from her feet so as to cool her, but she said to me: "Perhaps that is not allowed?" Mother Marie de Gonzague had told us once that even in summer it was better to keep on the wool blanket, and Sister Thérèse of the Child Jesus did not think herself dispensed by illness from practicing obedience and mortification. . . . She would only have had to say a word to have this relief that all those who are ill take anyway without even thinking that permission for it might be necessary. (Testimony of Sister Marie of the Sacred Heart, PO 253)

If Our Mother Threw It in the Fire?

She also said: "The manuscript [the story of her life] must be published without delay after my death."

I said to her: "So you think that it is through the manuscript that you will do good for souls?"

"Yes, that is the means that God will use to grant my wish. It will do good for all sorts of souls, except those who are on extraordinary paths."

"But," I added, "what if our mother were to throw it in the fire?"

"Well, I would not feel the least distress about it or have the least doubt about my mission. I would quite simply think that God would fulfill my desires by some other means." (Testimony of Mother Agnès, PO 176)

We were speaking together about the little attention that was paid to the practice of hidden virtues. [Thérèse responded:] "This struck me in the life of St. John of the Cross, about whom they said: 'Brother John of the Cross! He's a religious who is less than ordinary!'" (LC August 2, no. 2, p. 128)

We became aware only toward the end of her life that the cold, no doubt because of the state of her health, afflicted her in a particularly painful way. Yet we never saw her rubbing her hands in winter or doing anything that would lead us to suspect her suffering. She never said, "It's very cold" or "It's warm." She never complained of anything. One day, a Sister wanting to refasten the scapular of the Servant of God, pinned through both her skin and the material at the same time. Sister Thérèse of the Child Jesus let nothing show and continued her refectory work quite joyfully for several hours. But finally she was afraid, she said, "of no longer being in obedience . . ." and took the pin out of her shoulder. (Testimony of Mother Agnès, PO 168)

One day, when I had a violent headache, Sister Thérèse of the Child Jesus wanted me to go tell our Mother; since I objected, claiming that this would be a way of asking for relief, she said to me: "What would you say if you had been given the obligation I was, when I was a postulant and a novice? Our [novice] mistress ordered me to tell her every time I had a stomach ache. That happened every day, and this command became a veritable torture for me. Whenever I had a stomach ache, I would have preferred to suffer a hundred lashes rather than go tell her, but I did so every time out of obedience. Our mistress, who no longer remembered the order she had given me, would say: 'My poor child, you'll never have the health to keep the rule; it is too much for you.' Or else she would ask Mother Gonzague for some remedy for me, who would be annoyed and reply: 'For goodness sake, that child is always complaining! We come to Carmel to suffer; if she can't put up with her aches and pains, let her leave.' Nevertheless, out of obedience, I continued for a long time to confess my stomach aches, at the risk of being sent away, until God finally took pity on my weakness and permitted them to free me from the obligation to make this confession." (Testimony of Sister Marie of the Trinity, PO 465)

I Would Not Have Desired to Make Any Move

We have recalled above how, in January 1896, Mother Marie de Gonzague had "begun a campaign to have Sister Geneviève sent to the Carmel of Saigon" and had wanted to delay her date of profession "for reasons of jealousy". Thérèse did not hesitate to protest: "There are some forms of testing that one must not use." This gesture would be brought up at the process (cf. CG 2:1181–84).

On August 2, 1896, there was some question of Mother Agnès' departure for a mission Carmel; the context was entirely different. Thérèse explains it:

I accepted not only exile for myself among an unknown people, but also, and this was *far more bitter* for me, I accepted exile for my sisters. Never shall I forget August 2, 1896; that day was precisely the day of the missionaries' departure, and there was serious consideration of the departure of Mother Agnes of Jesus. Ah! I would not have desired to make any move to prevent her leaving; I felt, however, a great sadness in my heart. . . . Jesus was silent; He was giving no commands to the storm. I said to Him: My God, I accept everything out of love for You: if You will it, I really want to suffer even to the point of dying of grief. Jesus was content with this acceptance. However, a few months after this, they spoke of the departure of Sister Geneviève and Sister Marie of the Trinity. Then this was another kind of suffering, very intimate, very deep; I imagined all the trials, the disappointment they would suffer, and my heaven was covered with clouds; calm and peace remained only in the depths of my heart. (SS 216–17)

She never lost this strength, especially with regard to her sisters: "You must pay attention to regular observance. After a visit, don't stop to talk among yourselves, because then it's like being at home, and we deprive ourselves of nothing" (LC August 3, no. 6; p. 130). And: "After I'm gone, be very careful not to lead a family life, not to recount anything from your parlor visits without permission and yet only ask permission when these are very useful things" (DE 617). And she herself would be very careful in this, even to the point of knowingly paining her sister, Mother Agnès: she said nothing to her of her first hemoptyses for some fourteen months; she had given notice to her prioress; that was enough (LC May 30, no. 1); similarly, she would say nothing to her for two years about Father Roulland, the missionary confided to her as a spiritual brother (LC May 1, no. 2); likewise the trial of faith would remain hidden from her sisters (cf. SS 214).

Then, two months before dying, on July 29, rapidly growing worse, she would have the right to express herself:

A Sister reported this reflection made during recreation: "Why are they talking of Sister Thérèse as though she were a saint? She practiced virtue, true, but it wasn't a virtue acquired through

humiliations and especially sufferings." She said to [Mother Agnès]
afterwards:

"And I who suffered so much from my most tender childhood! Ah, how much good it does me to see the opinion of
creatures, especially at the moment of my death!" (LC July
29, no. 2, pp. 115–16, and PO 177)

This discretion was such that it seemed natural even at the
hardest of times. A message to Lisieux, on Sunday morning,
July 29, 1894, relayed the news of the death of M. Martin at
La Musse.

In the afternoon, Sister Marie of the Sacred Heart would
later recount, Mme. Maudelonde asked us to the parlor; I saw
again that poor little Thérèse; she was pale; she followed
behind us without saying anything; she said practically nothing in the parlor either; that was usual for her; they didn't pay
any attention to her because she was the little one. (Conversation of July 29, 1926; notebook of Sister Marie of the
Incarnation, p. 109; CG 2:780)

You Will Be Sent Away—I Know It

Keeping silent, moderating oneself to the point of putting
the other ahead of oneself does not mean not daring to speak
when it is necessary. One episode will suffice. It was at the
end of 1892. The three youngest in the Carmel were Thérèse,
the sacristan, Sister Marie-Madeleine, and Sister Marthe, the
cook. This latter, outgoing but not very intelligent, was excessively attached to the Mother Prioress, Mother Marie de
Gonzague, "as a dog is attached to its master" (SS 237).
Thérèse recounts, in the *Story of a Soul*, how, on December 8,
she undertook to fulfill her role of novice mistress and make
Sister Marthe understand that this attachment was exaggerated. But what she does not say, her Sister Agnès reveals: the

risk that Thérèse took that day. Thérèse had thus decided to
open the eyes of her overly attentive companion with respect
to Mother Marie de Gonzague. She measured the risks of this
step and confided it to Sister Agnès of Jesus. "Pray much for
me", she said to me in a grave tone. "The Blessed Virgin has
inspired me to enlighten Sister Marthe. I am going to say to
her tonight everything I'm thinking about her." "But you
risk being betrayed", I said to her. "Then our Mother won't
be able to stand you any more, and you'll be sent away to
another monastery." "I know it," she replied, "but since I am
certain now that it is my duty to speak, I must pay no attention to the consequences." [8]

Silence was not purchased, for her, at the expense of truth.
The *Last Conversations* give numerous proofs of this, always
bathed in that humor with which she accepted being only
what she was:

> *Sister Marie of the Sacred Heart told her that when she died the
> angels would come to her in the company of Our Lord, that she
> would see them resplendent with light and beauty:*
>
> "All these images do me no good; I can nourish myself on
> nothing but the truth. This is why I've never wanted any
> visions. We can't see, here on earth, heaven, the angels, etc.,
> as they are. I prefer to wait until after my death." (LC August
> 5, no. 4, p. 134)

"When I think of how much trouble I've had all my life
trying to recite the rosary!" (LC August 20, no. 16, p. 160).
She could say: "It is not the pain it appears to be (dying of
love), provided it is really it!" (LC July 14, no. 4, p. 97). "I tell
the whole truth, and if anyone doesn't wish to know the
truth, let her not come looking for me" (LC April 18, no. 3,
p. 38). "O my God, I really want to listen to You; I beg You

---

[8] CG 2:668; cf. SS 235–37; and the testimony of Sister Marthe, PO 430.

to answer me when I say humbly: What is truth? Make me see things as they really are. Let nothing cause me to be deceived" (LC July 21, no. 4, p. 105). And the day of her death: "I never sought anything but the truth" (LC September 30, p. 205). It is before this that Bernanos would bow:

Our heavenly friend will not want me to speak as a child. I am, alas!, only an old child burdened with inexperience, and you don't have much to fear from me. Dread those who are going to come, who will judge you, dread the innocent children, for they are also *enfants terribles*. The only side that remains for you to take is the one that the saint suggests to you, become children again yourselves, find once again the spirit of childhood. For the hour is coming when the questions that will be asked of you from all points of the earth will be so pressing and so simple that you will scarcely be able to reply to them except with a yes or no.

For a long time at evening meditation, I was placed in front of a Sister who had a strange habit and I think many lights because she rarely used a book during meditation. This is what I noticed: as soon as this Sister arrived, she began making a strange little noise which resembled the noise one would make when rubbing two shells, one against the other. I was the only one to notice it because I had extremely sensitive hearing (too much so at times). Mother, it would be impossible for me to tell you how much this little noise wearied me. I had a great desire to turn my head and stare at the culprit who was very certainly unaware of her "click." This would be the only way of enlightening her. However, in the bottom of my heart I felt it was much better to suffer this out of love for God and not to cause the Sister any pain. I remained calm, therefore, and tried to unite myself to God and to forget the little noise. Everything was useless. I felt the perspiration inundate me, and I was obliged simply to make a prayer of suffering; however, while suffering, I searched for a way of doing it without annoyance and with peace and joy, at least in the interior of my soul. I tried to love the little noise which was so displeasing; instead of trying not to hear it (impossible), I paid close attention so as to hear it well, as though it were a delightful concert, and my prayer . . . was spent in offering this concert to Jesus. (SS 249–50)

Those Who Can No Longer Speak

To sum up all these accounts and to specify what most manifests the simplicity of Thérèse, one expression suffices: the power of silence, as it was for Christ and the Virgin at Nazareth. At the beginning, this may have been for many motives: practical, devotional, a matter of obedience. It matters little. If it holds true for an entire life, one must indeed recognize that it comes from another kind of love. Someone had traced this path; Thérèse wanted to imitate it. But she was led still farther: as in a third stage, it was no longer a matter simply of mortifying herself or even of imitating Christ, but, because of the humiliations, it was a matter of agreeing merely to become part of the destitute, those who can no longer speak. She knew by heart the description in Isaiah 53. What she had read, she saw realized in her father, in herself.[9] She perceived the meaning of it: not only an invitation to imitate the hidden life of Nazareth, but a call to unite

[9] "There was more and more silence around the venerated name of the one we cherished. In the community where, up until then, he had enjoyed something like prestige, if his name was pronounced, it was in a whisper, like the name of a man almost dishonored" (Mother Agnès of Jesus, *Souvenirs intimes*, p. 83, CG 2:615). August 25 to September 30, 1897: too weak from then on to write and, soon, to speak, the sick Thérèse entered into silence. Others still wrote to her (LC 196 to 202). The last three letters, from China, Africa, and Canada, would not arrive in Lisieux until after her death (cf. CG 2:970).

herself to the One who had kept silence throughout his life about his divinity and who had known humiliation.

Silence, for her, revealed not only the presence of charity in all concrete life, in all the "virtues", but also how hope is the finest fruit of charity in a life. That is why we approach hope after charity. With Thérèse, silence became what, in the midst of the worst difficulties, best revealed her desire to leave the initiative to God. It was this absence of personal intervention in order to "arrange things" that Thérèse admired in the Virgin (silence with regard to Joseph, for example, in the poem "Saint Cecilia"; see PN3). The poetry of May 1897 (PN 54, "Why I Love You, O Mary!", stanza 8, lines 5–8) is perhaps the most indicative of this. Thérèse had grasped and formulated well the reversal of hope. As if silence alone could say to God: "It's your turn." It becomes all-powerful, for it shows that in accepting one's own limits to the end, and by keeping silent, one hopes all the same, like Daniel (3:17–18), like Job, like all who face the silence of God. . . . It is the moment of the "impossible step", of the final circle of hope. For Thérèse, apparently God "did not play" in the short term. She accepted then entering into the silence of the Suffering Servant, who called for help "with loud cries and tears" (Heb 5:7) and who was answered. "Your strength will lie in silence and hope", says the rule of Carmel.

The Silences of Thérèse

—On the death of her mother: "Without a word I placed my lips on her forehead. . . . Neither did I speak to anyone about the feelings I experienced. I looked and listened in silence" (SS 33).

—Her grandmother took away her bouquet of flowers: "This didn't please little Thérèse, but she kept from saying anything, having got into the habit of not complaining ever, even when . . . she was accused unjustly. She preferred to be silent and not excuse herself" (SS 30).

—First year of boarding school (SS 53; cf. PO 137): "Never to complain or excuse oneself."

—Lisieux, 1882–1883: "Ah! how I suffered from this *visit* to Carmel! . . Every Thursday we went *as a family* to Carmel and I . . . obtained with great trouble two or three minutes at the end of the visit. . . . I didn't understand and I said in the depths of my heart: 'Pauline is lost to me!'" (SS 60). "Ah! what I suffered I shall not be able to say except in heaven!" (SS 67).

—Headaches or "The Donkey and the Little Dog": "Marie [Guérin], who was almost always ailing, often *whimpered*. . . . I, who had a headache almost every day and didn't complain, wanted to imitate Marie. . . . I answered like Marie: 'I have a headache.' It seemed that complaining didn't suit me. . . . I understood the fable about *'The donkey and the pet dog.'* . . . I did get what I deserved and this cured me for life of any desire to attract attention" (SS 89–90).

—"My mortifications consisted . . . in holding back a reply, in rendering little services without any recognition" (SS 143).

—"Ah! I desired that, like the Face of Jesus, 'my face be truly hidden'" (SS 152).

—The little lamp: "One evening, after Compline, I was looking in vain for our lamp on the shelves reserved for this purpose. It was during the time of the Great Silence and so it was impossible to complain to anyone about my loss. I understood that a Sister, believing she was taking her lamp, picked up ours which I really needed. . . . I was really happy, feeling that Poverty consists in being deprived not only of agreeable things but of indispensable things too" (SS 159).

—The broken vase: "I was exerting much effort, too, at not excusing myself. . . . A little vase set behind a window was broken, and our Mistress, thinking it was my fault. . . . Without a word, I kissed the floor. . . . Because of my lack of virtue these little practices cost me very much. . . . I noticed this: when one performs her duty, never excusing herself, no one knows it; on the contrary, imperfections appear immediately" (SS 159).

—Silence with Sister Agnès (while working in the refectory): "I did not feel, *as formerly*, free to say everything to you, for there was the Rule to observe. I was unable to confide in you; after all, I was in *Carmel* and no longer at *Les Buissonnets* under the *paternal roof*!" (SS 160).

—For five years . . . "Yes, suffering opened wide its arms to me and I threw myself into them with love. . . . Exteriorly nothing revealed my suffering" (SS 149).

—Prayer of the "little noise" (SS 249–50); see above, pp. 196–97.

—Hemoptyses: for fourteen months, from April 1896 to May 1897, she said nothing of her hemoptyses to her sister, Mother Agnès (cf. LC May 30, no. 1).

—There was question of one of her sisters leaving for a mission Carmel (cf. SS 216–17). This caused her suffering, but she kept silent.

—September 1896 (after having remained in silence and dryness): "Do not believe I am swimming in consolations; oh, no, my consolation is to have none on earth. Without showing Himself, without making His voice heard, Jesus teaches me in secret" (SS 187).

—She experienced the trial of faith but hid it from her sisters (SS 210, 213-14).

—For two years, she said nothing to Mother Agnès about Father Roulland, the missionary who had been confided to her as a spiritual brother (LC May 1, no. 2, p. 41).

—Blessed silence: "When we're misunderstood and judged unfavorably, what good does it do to defend or explain ourselves? Let the matter drop and say nothing. It's so much better to say nothing and allow others to judge us as they please! We don't see in the Gospel where Mary explained herself. . . . No, she preferred to remain silent. O blessed silence" (LC April 6, no. 1, p. 36).

—June 1897: "They don't believe I'm as sick as I am. . . . As far as I am concerned, what does it matter what others think or say? I don't see why I should be disturbed about it" (LC June 12, pp. 63–64).

—Allowing what belongs to you to be taken without asking for it back: "Although it is difficult to give to one who asks, it is even more so *to allow one to take what belongs to you, without asking it back*" (SS 225).

—I haven't the right to complain when one takes a thing that is not mine: "Jesus does not want me to lay claim to what belongs to me. . . . I have renounced the goods of this earth through the Vow of Poverty, and so I haven't the right to complain when one takes a thing that is not mine. . . . We are acting like the poor who extend their hand to receive what is necessary for them; if they are rebuked they are not surprised, as no one owes them anything" (SS 226).

—"The goods of heaven . . . are *lent* to me by God, who can withdraw them without my having a right to complain" (SS 233).

—July 29, 1897: One Sister in the Carmel was surprised to hear others speaking of Thérèse as if she were a saint although she had not suffered. Thérèse was at the height of her illness, which was causing her agony. She said nothing in reply upon learning of this reflection and said merely: "How much good it does me to see the opinion of creatures, especially at the moment of my death!" (LC July 29, no. 2, pp. 115–16).

—"Take silence, for example, what good it does to the soul, what failures in charity it prevents, and so many other troubles of all kinds. I speak especially about silence because it's on this point that we fail the most" (LC August 6, no. 5, p. 137).

—One month before her death, she was suffering a great deal and groaned. "Little Mother! . . . Yes! . . . I want it! I must no longer complain; this is useless. Pray for me, little sisters, but not on your knees, seated" (LC August 22, no. 10, p. 164).

—Mother Agnès recalls: "*I was telling her she suffered less during the silence*: 'Oh! just the opposite! I suffered very much, very much! But it's to the Blessed Virgin that I complained'" (LC September 5, no. 3, p. 184; cf. also LC September 13, no. 1, p. 189).

—During the process, the allusions to silence were often placed under the titles "Fortitude" or "Prudence". The testimony of the other Sisters brought it up as often as Thérèse's own sisters as a dominant characteristic of her attitude. Note, besides what we have just cited: Sister Thérèse of Saint Augustine: "She never excused herself" (PO 402); Sister Marie-Madeleine: "I also noticed how silent she was" (PO 480); Sister Marie of the Angels on the subject of the cold (PO 416), and so on.

*

All the facts we have just recalled are sufficient to describe the secret heroism of Thérèse of Lisieux hidden behind the power of her silence. This identification, however, is not sufficient to indicate the message of that silence.

All silence is frightening because it contains a certain image of death. "The silence of space frightens"; it is normal, and how is it possible to accept when it's a matter of one's death? The silence of Christ indicates that, between the silence of emptiness and the silence of fright, there is another kind. There are not merely two terms, but three. If the first type of silence is a trial, and if another is repose, there is also a silence that can nourish and end in communion. Every human being is in reality a solitary being, but a solitary being who is loved and is both dependent on a love in order to exist and in expectation of that love. Step by step, Thérèse transformed her anxiety, her solitude, and the anguish of silence into prayer. She challenged God. Humanity cannot get out of it. In the depth of her silence, Thérèse discovered that she had been invited, and that it was irrevocable—for God had decided it from all eternity—to go back to her original vocation: to be this eternal need for love, for truth, for communion (cf. Eph 1). It was a question for her of going back to the principle of her life, her first state, the very one that constituted her: that communion with God, that attachment she was not afraid to call by the name of mystical "wedding", in and through the prayer of Jesus.

Audacity is not only legitimate here but necessary. In Jesus, it is not only God (or a god) who becomes incarnate, but the Word of the Father. The God of Thérèse is not monolithic, not solitary; he is Trinity. In him, the Three are totally related one to the other. The Son who is Word has reality only through his relation to his Father, to the One who engenders and utters him. Silence is thus constitutive of his very being. It is through and in silence first of all that the Word is "with the Father", according to the expression of Saint John and the Epistle to the Hebrews, so often taken up by the liturgy and predominant in the thought of Saint John of the Cross.

It is difficult, not to understand, but to admit. Van Gogh, Picasso, and Rubens exhausted themselves expressing their word in seven hundred or twenty-five hundred paintings. They exhausted themselves and never did manage to express what they were. God has only one Son, who is his Word, and he is an "only" Son, with all the pathos this term assumes for human beings. It is in silence that this Word says all that He is. Following Christ, it was through silence, more than through words, that prayer placed Thérèse in contact with God.

CHAPTER SEVENTEEN

I Have Seen a Saint Die—
It Is Not What You Imagine

"I have seen a saint die—I who am speaking to you—and it is not what you imagine; it is not like what you read in books: you must hold firm in the face of it; you feel the armor of the soul crack." So said Bernanos with respect to Thérèse of Lisieux.

"Even death", was it so for Thérèse of Lisieux? Was she preserved from fear, from anxiety? She did not know how she would do; several times she questioned in the course of the last six months: "I wonder how I will do when dying. I would like, nevertheless, to come off 'with honor!' But I believe this doesn't depend on oneself" (LC June 6, no. 3, p. 58). And another day, she was still more destitute: "What must I do to die? Never will I know how to die!" (LC September 29, no. 2, p. 201). Believing her strong and determined in the face of death, those around her attributed that to the illusions of youth and told her that she would be afraid; then she replied quite simply: "This could very well be true. . . . I never rely on my own ideas. . . . However, I want to rejoice in the feeling that God gives me at the present moment. There will always be time to suffer the opposite" (LC May 20, no. 1, p. 46).

It is possible to note the difference between Thérèse's attitude toward death and that of her sisters; it was clear at the
time of the influenza epidemic, in January 1892; Thérèse was
nineteen years old at the time (cf. her account, SS 171–72);
here is the report given in the monastery's chronicle:

> The influenza epidemic raged in our region with force. On
> December 28, Holy Innocents, several of our Sisters had to
> take to their beds. When we saw our good Sister St. Joseph,
> eighty-three, seized by this terrible sickness, we had no doubt
> that the Lord would find her ripe for heaven. We then
> mourned the departure of Mother Subprioress, Sister Fébro-
> nie of the Holy Childhood, and Sister Madeleine: three
> coffins in less than eight days! . . . Our Reverend Mother was
> very sick, all our Sisters confined to bed; never in the annals
> of our Carmel had we seen the like. At the burial of our two
> Sisters, hardly six or seven were present, and then at the cost
> of a great effort on their part! Only the three youngest of the
> entire Community were not stricken by this epidemic. . . .
> What Community life! No more office in choir, no prayer,
> no reading in the refectory, no bells rung for religious exer-
> cises. Death was hanging over us!" (Foundation 3, p. 206; GC
> 2:747, n. 1)

It was, moreover, in the face of this attitude on Thérèse's
part, in January 1892, that Canon Delatroëtte, superior of the
Carmel, would change his opinion about her and lay down
his arms (cf. GC 2:1017).

As her own death approached, it was believed that she had
consolations because she still took it upon herself to compose
poems.

Her sisters and companions would testify to that giant
battle, eighteen months "in the tunnel and in darkness"; she
experienced the trial of faith.

If you only knew what frightful thoughts obsess me! Pray very much for me in order that I do not listen to the devil who wants to persuade me about so many lies. It's the reasoning of the worst materialists which is imposed upon my mind. . . . O little Mother, must one have thoughts like this when one loves God so much! . . . [*She added that she never reasoned with these thoughts:*] I undergo them under duress, but while undergoing them I never cease making acts of faith. (LC 257–58)

Sister Marie of the Trinity would testify:

Sister Thérèse of the Child Jesus had to submit to terrible temptations against faith. One day when she told me of the darkness in which her soul was, I said to her in complete surprise: "But those luminous canticles you composed contradict what you're telling me!" She replied: "I sing, but it is without any feeling. I would not even wish to tell you how dark the night is in my soul for fear of making you share in my temptations. (PA 131, cf. SS 214)

And Sister Thérèse of Saint Augustine: "She confided something to me that really surprised me. 'If you only knew', she said to me, 'into what darkness I am plunged! I don't believe in eternal life; it seems to me that after this mortal life there is nothing. Everything has disappeared for me' " (PO 402; cf. LC 268). At the height of the struggle, fear was not absent. She did not stop there. Her secret was elsewhere. To her sisters she repeated: "Don't be troubled, little sisters, if I suffer very much and if you see in me, as I've already said, no sign of happiness at the moment of my death. Our Lord really died as a Victim of Love, and you see what his agony was!" (LC June 4, no. 1, p. 56). She would take up the same idea again: To be ready to die, as a soldier of Christ, was not what one imagined: "Our Lord died on the Cross in agony, and yet this is the most beautiful death of love. This was the only one that was seen. . . . To die of love is not to die in transports" (LC July 4, no. 2, p. 73). There were no "transports", consolations, or ecstasy. You have here a young woman of twenty-four years of age. One year earlier, after the first hemoptysis of Good Friday, she had very well understood that the sign risked being decisive. Her health improved. But one year later, after Lent, the illness took total hold. On July 30, it was thought she would not last the night. Robust, she would not die until September 30.

The Regime of the "Confectioners"

Nothing can better release Thérèse from the regime of the "confectioners", according to Bernanos' expression, than the simple details about what she experienced in submitting to the treatments of the period, which were, alas, the only remedies of the time and what Professor Marrou describes as "ineffectual barbarisms". Let us merely cite two examples.

During the month of April 1897, after the return of her illness, Thérèse would endure four vesicatory sessions. Her sisters would be frightened at having to make her submit to such treatments. What is there to say?

In a book preserved in the Lisieux Carmel, having once belonged to Céline and which Thérèse may have had in hand at Les Buissonnets, we find these practical details:

> *Vesciatories.* When a vesicatory of the form and dimensions prescribed by the doctor has been procured, it is sprinkled with camphor, put for a moment in the fire, and then applied on the desired part of the body; then it is pressed a little with the hand, then covered with a light compress of fine cloth, and the whole fixed with a bandage or a napkin. . . . When the vesicatory has produced its effect, when the skin is swollen, the napkin is taken off with care, and the plaster is lifted

off gently, beginning with a corner. And the blister is ex-
posed. Then it is pierced with scissors at the lowest part and
the matter allowed to drain. If the vesicatory is not to be
sustained, the wound is dressed with an ointment of fresh
butter placed as a thin layer on fine linen. To dry it, some
powdered starch or some potato starch is placed on the
wound. If the wound needs to be drained, epispastic paper,
which can be found at a pharmacy, is used. When the wound
is inflamed or irritated, this painful irritation can be treated
with a poultice of linseed powder. At each dressing, it is
useful to clean the wound with a fine piece of cloth. If, by
chance, the linen that covers the wound sticks to it, it should
be moistened with warm water before being removed. A
vesicatory can remain in place five or six hours for a child,
twelve hours or more with adults.

Two letters from Mme. Zélie Martin also mention vesicatories:

I am worried about my little Thérèse; she has difficulty in
breathing for several months and this is not natural. As soon as
she walks quickly, I hear a strange whistling in her chest. I
consulted a doctor, he told me to give her an emetic; I did it
and she is even worse. I think a vesicatory would do her some
good, but it is frightening to think of it. (November 12, 1876,
GC 2:1227)

My little Thérèse is sick, and I am worried about it. She has
frequent colds giving her breathing problems. This lasts usually two days. I must consult the doctor, but he will tell me to
give her vesicatories and that frightens me. (January 8, 1877,
GC 2:1229; cf. DE 798–99)

Another notation from her sister Geneviève:

I still see her suffering more than five hundred punctures from
a hot needle on her back (I myself counted them). While the
doctor was at work, talking all the while to our Mother about

ordinary things, the angelic patient was standing, leaning
against a table. She told me later that she offered her sufferings
for souls and thought of the martyrs. After the session, she
went up to her cell without waiting for a word of compassion
from anyone, sat down on the edge of her poor straw mattress, trembling all over, and there endured alone the effect of
that painful treatment. When evening came, since she was
not yet considered to be seriously ill, there could be no
question of a mattress, so the only choice I had was to fold
our blanket in four and slip it over her straw mattress, which
my poor little Sister accepted with gratitude, without letting
a single word of criticism escape her lips about the primitive
way the sick were cared for at that time.

It is true that in the midst of the most acute suffering, she
maintained great serenity and gaity. Inwardly, I was surprised
by it, thinking that it was because she was not suffering as
much as we thought, and I wanted to catch her in some
moment of crisis. A little later, I saw her smile and asked her
why. She said to me: "It's because I feel a very sharp pain in
my side, and I've made it a point always to welcome suffering
eagerly." (CSG 172–73)

For the whole history of Thérèse's illness, the reader should
refer to the book of our friend and companion Guy Gaucher,
The Passion of Thérèse of Lisieux.[1] This was, along with the
doctoral thesis of Father Descouvemont on the charity of
Thérèse of Lisieux and the important study on the *Dynamique
de la confiance* [Dynamic of trust] by Father Conrad De Meester, the first work of true renewal in Thérèsian history, ap-
pearing on the occasion of the centenary of her birth. The
reader should also refer to the *Derniers entretiens*[2] and the *Correspondance générale.*[3]

[1] Trans. Sister Anne Marie Brennan (New York: Crossroad, 1998).
[2] *Derniers entretiens* (Cerf/DDB, 1871), pp. 23–32, 132–46, 795–808.
[3] Vol. 2, pp. 968–70 and especially pp. 1188–93.

It is not necessary to recall the results of the illness for
Thérèse: gangrene in the intestines and the psychic suspen-
sion of waiting, for days and days, in the distress of utter
darkness of faith.

I Am Not Protected More Than Anyone Else

Thérèse lived this obstacle course with a sense of humor,
a sweetness, and a delicacy that leave us, like Bernanos,
speechless.

"It's not 'death' that will come in search of me, it's God.
Death isn't some phantom, some horrible spectre, as it is
represented in pictures" (LC May 1, no. 1, p. 41). "Oh! little
sisters, how happy I am! I see that I'm going to die very soon"
(LC June 4, no. 1, p. 55). And one day when the confessor
asked her if she was resigned to die, she replied: "Ah! Father,
I find I need resignation only to live. For dying, it's only joy
I experience" (LC June 6, no. 2, p. 58). That does not prevent
her from being ready for everything, for fear as well as for joy:
"Why should I be protected more than anyone else from the
fear of death? I won't say like St. Peter: 'I will never deny
you' " (LC July 9, no. 6, p. 83). She would be impatient for it:
"I do not count on the illness, it is too slow a leader. I *count
only on love*" (LT 242, GC 2:1121). At that moment, however,
she still had more than three months to live. Two months later
she would say: "God has done what He willed to do. . . . He
will come like a thief at an hour when no one is thinking of
Him; that's my idea" (LC July 31, no. 16, p. 124). And one
week before her death, when someone said to her: "What a
terrible sickness and how much you're suffering!", she replied, "Yes! What a grace it is to have faith! If I had not had
any faith, I would have committed suicide without an instant's
hesitation" (LC September 22, no. 6, p. 196).

From Now On

Thérèse had already encountered death: that of her mother, that of her father, and entering Carmel was a kind of death to all that she was leaving. But the confrontation between faith and death is something else: more profound and closer. Thérèse understood that death is not only something that awaits us later, something that will arrive only at the end of our life. No, every day we live in a condition in which everything is fragile, friable, fleeting, in which things and beings are passing. "Things are passing, things die in our life at every moment." The word concordance shows how frequent this word is with Thérèse: more than eighty-one times in her letters, of which sixty-four have a temporal sense: life, time, the world are . . . passing. It does indeed dominate her thought.

Thérèse is one with today's philosophers when they define man as a "being made for death", that is, the only animal capable of situating at every moment the things that are passing on a horizon that is not. Thérèse's first conclusion is simple: If "things are passing", there is one single reality that counts, the one that is at hand, the one by which we escape from now on the reach of death: it is the present moment. Nothing of it must be lost, since it allows us to join the end immediately and, because of that, to make small things to be like the great and thus to conquer death (LT 108, GC 1:629; LT 85, p. 546; LT 89, p. 556; and so on).

There is a second conclusion: Death is the most inescapable event, the one that dominates us, in the face of which we are the most disarmed, and that is why we mobilize everything in order to hide it. We no longer die, we are "deceased". We hide death as if there were nothing more obscene.

Thérèse proved that it is possible to do something else besides suffer it.

Bernanos, who was an expert, was not fooled:

> "Oh! Mother, is this the end?" said the little Saint Thérèse during her agony to her prioress. "What must I do to die! . . ." Joan of Arc must have thought like that on the morning of May 30, 1429. What charms our soul in this childlike expression is precisely that it does not defy death but, on the contrary, welcomes it with a kind of discreet shyness and as if with a fear of displeasing it. Here we recognize the perfection of a kind of heroism of which we are more or less aware of being the servants and witnesses. What does it matter if this is a child's remark! It is to such child's remarks that men rise. [4]

I Am Entering into Life

> I have frequently noticed that Jesus doesn't want me to lay up *provisions*; He nourishes me at each moment with a totally new food; I find it within me without my knowing how it is there. I believe it is Jesus Himself hidden in the depths of my poor little heart: He is giving me the grace of acting within me, making me think of all He desires me to do at the present moment. (SS 165)

> No, God gives me no premonition of an approaching death, but of much greater sufferings. . . . But I don't torment myself, I don't want to think of anything but the present moment. (LC August 23, no. 3, p. 165)

With Thérèse, the itinerary of every man appears indeed as a real, although infinitesimal, segment of the curve traced by the whole of history from year to year, those years that are given for working, those years, too, in which the work

---

[4] Georges Bernanos, *Lettre aux Anglais* (Paris: Gallimard, 1946), pp. 28–29.

of grace deepens; from year to year those words of the apostle become literally more true: "Salvation is nearer to us now than when we first believed" (Rom 13:11). The progress of time moves imperceptibly closer to that final hour, as unforeseeable as that of the "end of the world" when, our concrete participation in the work of history having been accomplished, we will leap beyond time to the feet of the sovereign Judge; and consequently something of the gravity of that hour is outlined on each of our moments. With Thérèse of Lisieux, that truth tends to receive a deeper meaning. The last day is not only one moment in the chain of time, one set day out of a year that will bear her date according to the era in force with historians of that time; it is also the fact of the total fulfillment of God's design for his creature. If that fulfillment will be achieved only on that famous day, it would be wrong to imagine that it is wholly reserved for that future: in reality, that fulfillment accompanies and sustains the progress of each instant; it is present and gathers the fruit of every tear and of every impulse of love. It is the whole of time that comes, in that way, to take on a participation in the "eschatological" quality, in a literally true sense, of an anticipation, of a foretaste, of a beginning of eternal life.

Time must be filled with activity. Make "the most of time, because the days are evil", says Ephesians 5:16. In Colossians 4:5, *exagarazesthai* means rather "exhaust the occasions", "draw out the best part" of that time we have been given to live; "while it is day" (Jn 9:4), it is time to accomplish the works of light, illuminated as we are by the sun of justice. In some way, each time, the apostolic words become a little more literally true, more directly applicable: "The night is far gone, the day is at hand" (Rom 13:12); "I mean, brethren, the appointed time has grown very short" (1 Cor 7:29); "For yet a little while" (Heb 10:37); "The end of all things is at hand" (1 Pet 4:7); "Children, it is the last hour" (1 Jn 2:18); "Surely I am coming soon" (Rev 22:20).

*

"I really don't see what I'll have after death that I don't already possess in this life. I shall see God, true; but as far as being in His presence, I am totally there here on earth" (LC May 17, no. 7, p. 45). For Thérèse, everything had already begun. "How sad life is", moaned a Sister close to her. Thérèse replied: "No, life is not sad, it is the exile that is sad." She concluded: "I am not dying, I am entering into life."

CHAPTER EIGHTEEN

Childhood and Oblation

Why Thérèse of Lisieux?

Thérèse's little way of childhood is a way of supreme courage, that of truth. In restoring to us the true face of God, of that mercy which re-creates splendor, *because* of our fragility, and of the reciprocity that disarms straight off, by inducing us to choose that mercy to the very end, Saint Thérèse recalls the secret of the true glory of God, that of the mercy that responds to trust, that of reciprocal love.

Faith and hope are not love. Saint Paul has spelled that out well. Thérèse of Lisieux helps us understand that the finest gift of love that we can make to God is confidence born of faith and hope. In its poverty and its nothingness, confidence is indeed the only thing the creature can offer to God. It is its own gift, its precious stone. Thérèse knew that this confidence offered by men is still more precious than that of the angels, for men are immersed in misery and weakness. Their confidence rests on a presentiment of mercy that is more profound than that of the angels. That is why Saint Paul says that faith justifies and that it is vain to seek in our works for gifts that would be more brilliant and more important than this confidence. Saint Thérèse had understood that the martyr himself would be nothing without this confidence. She knew that any possibility of an offering is a gift that God makes us. By permitting us to offer, God responds to the confident, happy, and, dare we say, "blind" fidelity of our lives as poor sinners, as beings who are at times without hope and who rightly have nothing more to offer than to hold firm "against all hope", according to the expression of Saint Paul, following Abraham. Like Jesus during the agony, like Mary at the foot of the Cross, like Thérèse in her illness, every place where God asks us to be, God knows that we will always have to offer him this infinitely precious gift of confidence, that which Thérèse called, when writing to her favorite novice, Sister Marie of the Trinity: "the silver of childlike simplicity".

This is not yet the gold of charity. Nor is it yet the burst of love that God gives his saints, but it is the gift of their confidence, in a poverty that at times groans in its state of destitution. This silver of simplicity is that of the way of childhood. It enhances the garland of love that God himself places around our necks. In asking his Father: "Why have you abandoned me?" Jesus has placed his soul in the hands of his Father in that indescribable confidence that animates the faith of Mary, of the Church, and of the saints. Once again it is the sole gift that we can make to God.

And this gift is real enough to make God beg for this confidence. Each time we avoid or refuse it, we wound the trinitarian presence, the Holy Spirit in the depths of us, to such an extent that, to make us suspect what we are thus doing to God at that moment, the Father found nothing better than to send Jesus to earth, asking him to extend his beautiful arms on the Cross. It was indeed before the beloved Christ that Thérèse would offer to the Holy Trinity her hands, perhaps empty, but full of the most beautiful fruit of her love: her confidence.

> O My God! Most Blessed Trinity, I desire to *Love* You and make You *Loved*. . . . I desire to accomplish Your will perfectly. . . . I desire, in a word, to be a saint, but I feel my helplessness and I beg You, O my God! to be Yourself my *Sanctity*!
>
> Since You loved me so much as to give me Your only Son as my Savior and my Spouse, the infinite treasures of His merits are mine. I offer them to You with gladness, begging You to look upon me only in the Face of Jesus. . . .
>
> I am certain, then, that You will grant my desires; I know, O my God! that *the more You want to give, the more You make us desire*. . . .
>
> In the evening of this life, I shall appear before You with empty hands, for I do not ask You, Lord, to count my works. . . . I want no other . . . *Crown* but *You*, my *Beloved*! . . .
>
> I OFFER MYSELF AS A VICTIM OF HOLOCAUST TO YOUR MERCIFUL LOVE, . . . until the shadows having disappeared I may be able to tell You of my *Love* in an *Eternal Face to Face*! (SS 276–77)

CONCLUSION

Perfect Joy

Of course, there is the Joy of God, Joy per se—each of us has
his own idea of it. . . . But the saints, the very great saints,
keep the secret of letting it appear undamaged for the next.
What was I supposed to do in this human struggle? I suc-
ceeded only in easy things. And because I never tried anything else, others imagine that everything is possible for me;
they would like miracles from me. . . .

And as unfortunate as I might be one day, sadness will have
no part in me, ever. . . . Sin, that is what we all are inside,
some in order to enjoy it, others to suffer from it, but in the
end, it is the same bread that we break at the edge of the
fountain, holding our breath, the same distaste. Without
doubt you were wrong to expect something of me. But I give
you what I have, the little I have, neither more nor less. I no
longer want to defend myself, that's over. We don't have the
right to defend ourselves. . . . God doesn't keep any of us like
a precious bird, in a cage. He frees his best friends; he gives
them away for nothing to the good, to the bad, to the whole
world, just as he was given away by Pilate! "Look, watch,
here is the man."

Is Bernanos "reasoning falsely", as Sartre would say, on this
page of *La Joie*, where, secretly, he is only making Thérèse of
Lisieux speak, as so often in his work?

*

Thérèse was sent to the world as a sign from God, we said in our introduction, at a time when it is no longer mere weakness or culpability but solitude that afflicts humanity. Man is in a state of total destitution, alone with his freedom facing a God who has resigned his power: there is nothing left for him to do but expect the unexpected from this God. It was in the specifically metaphysical sadness of modern times that Thérèse, through the mysterious design of providence, had, among others, the vocation of taking on everything beneath an appearance of joy and consolation. This "appearance" of joy, which it seems only very rarely deserted her, was perhaps simply an enclosure that she raised between herself and others in order to remain alone in the darkness with the mysterious Beggar. "I truly want to suffer without saying so / That Jesus may be consoled" (PN 45, "My Joy", January 21, 1897, PST 186). In the most joyous pages of her manuscripts, of the *Last Conversations*, or of the *Letters*, Thérèse seeks to make us forget, through her spirit of humility, the depths into which she is drawn when she writes that one must dry the tears of Jesus by suffering with him "without courage", "with sadness".

Thérèse had occasion, in 1889, to speak twice in less than a month of an "unfelt joy, above all joy". It was first in letter 85, of March 12, where she announces to Céline that we shall be "deified at the very fountain of all joys, all delights" (GC 1:546); then in letter 87 of April 4, where she likens this "unfelt joy" to peace. "I found the secret of suffering in peace", she writes, "it is enough to will all that Jesus wills" (GC 1:553). In reality, it is a question of something that is above all joy and all suffering. That peace of the depths is the joy of God, the beginning of our deification in the "shadows of exile", the ineffable.

Going Back to the Source

To compose the history of Thérèse of Lisieux, several unify-
ing threads are necessary: charity, confidence, prayer, desire
for God. We must be attentive to the continuity and discon-
tinuity of her attitude toward her surroundings, to which she
has quickly been either set in opposition or reduced. We must
start all over again with each decisive moment: whether the
Christmas conversion, the novitiate, the encounter with
Scripture, the illness of her father, the Act of Oblation, the
trial of faith. On each occasion, everything begins again.
Everything was foreshadowed. As for each sacrament, everything is given, and everything remains to be done. It is always
difficult to resist the temptation of schematizing or stopping
short at sociocultural comparisons, as if one could say:
"Claudel = Aeschylus + Shakespeare", or "Thérèse = Jean de
Bernière (a spiritual writer who wrote on the spirit of childhood in the seventeenth century) + John of the Cross", or
"Thérèse: she is Anti-Pauline or Anti-Céline". But the saints
are mischievous. Thérèse was gifted. To those who would
like to believe that she despised the world, that she was a
victim of an erroneous dualism, or that she was tense about
her virginity, and so on, Thérèse has nothing to say. She
hides. Not in order to escape, but in order to oblige us to go
farther back, to the source, to that which dominates all of us:
the search for happiness.

Always Cheerful and Content

Just before the return of the worst hemoptyses, on July 5,
1897, she said to her sister Agnès: "Don't be sad about seeing
me sick, little Mother, for you can see how happy God makes
me. I'm always cheerful and content" (LC 74).

In point of fact, Thérèse did not know immediately how to transform her sufferings into joy. She explained herself in this respect very clearly on July 31, 1897. Some time after her First Communion, she had asked the Lord to transform all earthly consolation into bitterness for her. This prayer, which she had drawn from the Imitation of Christ, had been inspired by her fear of going to seek in the applause and affection of the "world" a joy that she wanted to find in God alone. She did not have long to wait for an answer: the friendship she was showing for some classmate was not returned, and many other trials came to descend upon her. Here is one of the most revealing confidences she shared:

> I have found happiness and joy on earth, but solely in suffering, for I've suffered very much here below; you must make it known to souls. . . .
>
> Since my First Communion, since the time I asked Jesus to change all the consolations of this earth into bitterness for me, I had a perpetual desire to suffer. I wasn't thinking, however, of making suffering my joy; this is a grace that was given to me later on. Up until then, it was like a spark hidden beneath the ashes, and like blossoms on a tree that must become fruit in time. But seeing my blossoms always falling, that is, allowing myself to fall into tears whenever I suffered, I said to myself with astonishment and sadness: But I will never go beyond the stage of desires! (LC July 31, no. 13, p. 123)

Later, Thérèse understood that, in order to suffer "according to the heart of God", there was no need to suffer with courage without seeming to notice her sufferings, like heroes and "great souls"; it was enough to accept her sufferings such as they were and such as she was, offering them to the Lord with all her heart and believing deeply that they were not useless. Thérèse had understood this perfectly from reading the notes taken by Sister Marie of Saint Joseph during a retreat preached by Father Pichon at the Lisieux Carmel in October 1887. The meditation on the agony of Christ ended with this conclusion: "God preserve us, said one saint, from suffering grandly, strongly, generously! Ah! Without that inner cross of discouragement, as we know, all the others would be nothing." Thérèse wrote to her sister Céline for her twentieth birthday, on April 26, 1889: "Let us not believe we can love without suffering, without suffering much. . . . Let us suffer the bitter pain, without courage! . . . (Jesus suffered in *sadness*! Without sadness would the soul suffer! . . .) And still we would like to suffer generously, grandly! . . . Céline! what an illusion!" (LT 89, GC 1:557).

It was truly in this way that Thérèse welcomed suffering on her infirmary bed. Suffering found her without strength, without joy, but what did it matter! As she had already foreseen when she was seventeen years old: "Sanctity does not consist in saying beautiful things, it does not even consist in thinking them, in feeling them! . . . It consists in *suffering* and suffering *everything*" (LT 89, GC 1:557–58).

Am I Suffering Well?

Thérèse never asked God to increase her sufferings: she was content to accept with a smile those that occurred. Witness this conversation of August 26, 1897, related by Sister Marie of the Eucharist in a letter to her father: "She was saying yesterday: 'Fortunately I didn't ask for suffering. If I had asked for it, I fear I wouldn't have the patience to bear it. Whereas, if it is coming directly from God's will, He cannot refuse to give me the patience and the grace necessary to bear it'" (LC 290; cf. also August 26, no. 2, p. 169).

One day Mother Agnès congratulated her on her patience.

Thérèse replied to her: "I haven't even one minute of patience. It's not my patience! You're always wrong!" (LC August 18, no. 4, p. 153).

"This isn't like persons who suffer from the past or the future; I myself suffer only at each present moment. So it's not any great thing" (LC 241). Thérèse admitted this on the day when, breaking down with anguish and temptations, she knew that from then on she would never be able to receive Communion (cf. LC August 20, no. 10, p. 157). Two days earlier she had said "I'm suffering very much, but am I suffering very well? That's the point!" (LC August 18, no. 1, p. 152). She had written at the end of the Gospels that she carried constantly with her: "Lord, you fill me with joy by all that you do" (Ps 16:5).

*

We cannot keep from protesting here: Does God need so many sufferings to make a saint? Is this not the question underlying Sartre's repugnance when he wrote: "Sanctity repels me, with its sophisms, is rhetoric, and its morose delights; it has but one single use today: to permit men of bad faith to reason falsely." [1]

Thérèse has answered. For her, it was not a question of suffering or not suffering, but of keeping the sweetness of love, the peace of love throughout everything (in LT 89 to Céline, she underlines the word *everything*). Christ on the Cross is, of course, a "tortured" man, but he is above all the one who loves his Father and men. If Jesus was crucified, it was not in order to make us crucified as well. It was in order to make us children.

[1] Jean-Paul Sartre, *Saint Genet, comédien et martyr* (Paris: Gallimard, 1970), pp. 227–30.

It Is a Sin to Renounce Happiness

It is unavoidable, legitimate, and obligatory to seek happiness. It is what Thérèse did all her life. But we can go in the wrong direction. For it is not immediately obvious that our true happiness lies in our conformity with the will of God.

Happiness is the possession, at once intense and peaceful, of all that we can desire. *Peace and intensity*: it is undoubtedly the union of these two words that makes the irreducible quality of happiness. It is at once gentle and violent. If one of the two notes is lacking, it is no longer happiness. A life can be filled with satisfaction without being happy, or perfectly peaceful and calm but without any happiness. Life, a pouring forth, inspiration, madness, and at the same time wisdom, security, gentleness, interiority, such are the two aspects of happiness. Movement and repose at one and the same time. This is really why it seems so often irreconcilable. We are tempted to choose one way or the other: adventure or equilibrium. Whence the two temptations, the two nostalgias of happiness: on the one hand, there are all the Don Juans and the Fausts, the lovers or the men of action who hope for happiness in adventure or in travel, indeed, in the feverishness of action, love, art, drugs. We must always be setting off. Even if it means asking death itself, as Baudelaire did, to take us away somewhere in order to find something new. On the other hand, we seek happiness in the security of an equilibrium, the assurance of a stable possession, the "joys of the hearth", and so on. And it is true: that does give happiness. Is it enough?

Even if men instinctively orient themselves toward one of the two faces of happiness, they all need both, and there is no happiness without both. Those who are on the road are tormented by the thirst of finding a reality, an object the possession of which will permit them finally to come to rest without losing the taste for intensity and novelty. Those who love order and repose wish for a fruitful, living calm, not drowsiness and sleep. Each has the need—admitted or not—of an ever-new life that is restful because simple and intense because infinite. Whence the disappointment—which will take the form of a cross—when we discover that we cannot satisfy ourselves with a created object, unless by forgetting either its limits or the greatness of our thirst. "God makes promises through his creatures and keeps them only through himself alone", wrote the young Claudel, the same year Thérèse entered the novitiate. The adventurers forget the limits by deafening themselves through the increasingly rapid replacement of the objects of their satisfaction. The first impact reveals the splendor in front of the frontiers. There is indeed that instant of "grace" when we can forget the limits and give ourselves the illusion of the infinite. . . . It is enough to change fruit each time we have drawn out the sugar from it. As for the others, they forget their thirst by settling too easily for a small-scale happiness. They are willing to compromise the real grandeur of their lives in order not to be weary any more, even it means justifying themselves through a virtuous stoicism in the face of life's sadnesses. To the end, Thérèse accepted the thirst for happiness . . . and she proclaimed that it is a sin for a Christian to renounce happiness.

The Surrender of the Heart

This was one of the most vibrant and original aspects of Thérèse of Lisieux; her instinct of faith kept her from fatal error here: to present cross and trial as external to happiness itself. It is obvious that the cross is on the path of happiness, but it seems as though *coming from outside*, as if ahead, blocking the road. Thérèse was more simple: her "happiness" was to love Someone, to love everyone. Because of that, she could suffer everything and be happy, if not on the surface, at least for what was essential.

Thérèse distinguished between the mystery of the cross and the mystery of our reception of divine life. This latter is much less terrifying for our imagination, but in reality it is the one formidable mystery, because in the final analysis our salvation and our acceptance of the cross itself depend on it. It is not the trial that is formidable, it is deciding whether or not to receive, to accept, to love to the end, the life that God proposes. It was not the cross that Judas refused; it was to yield in the face of the pardon. It is no longer a question of being strong but of being humble enough for love to triumph in our life. Now our strength depends much less on us than does our humility, than does our weakness; that was Thérèse's secret, the secret of the Beatitudes. The cross is not the true difficulty; rather it is the surrender of self through which we give ourselves to God.[2]

Any offer of a new life is frightening: it is always a leap into the unknown, what Thérèse would call at each stage: "shadows", "fog". And as attractive as that unknown might be, there is always a critical moment, precisely that of "passage", of the passover from one life to another, that moment when one loses the securities of the first without yet having those

[2] In the edition of *Maximes et avis spirituels de saint Jean de la Croix* that Thérèse often consulted (cf. GC 2:953–54, n. 2; LC 245–46), we find on p. 87, Counsel 307: "What you desire most and what you seek with the most solicitude, you will be able to attain by yourself, not through the highest contemplation, but through a more profound humility and through abasement of the heart." We can perhaps regret a certain dullness in the translation Thérèse had; the text, which is actually stronger, could be translated—and this is still closer to her intuition: "You will not arrive at what you require—and what you desire most—by your own path—or by high contemplation—but through a great humility and surrender of the heart [*y rendimiento de corazó*]."

of the second. In Dostoyevsky's *A Raw Youth*, in the dialogue between Catherine Nicolayevna and Versiloff—"Did you love me?" "Yes." "And now?" "No . . . I would perhaps have loved you if you had loved me less."—Catherine does not realize that she has just revealed the secret of their history. She is right. That man could offer her only security. God offers a life made of both the infinite and repose. How can we have both kinds of happiness? Being willing to receive the gospel is being willing to enter into another order of existence: a life that becomes our life by remaining essentially the life of another. In this perspective, we perceive that the Beatitudes can be understood only if we are already *in* the kingdom. This is their paradox: They propose happiness by opposing not only false human wisdom but also true wisdom (1 Cor 1:17 and 2:9). They have their justification only in being fulfilled in God.

Everything seems ordained in the Gospels to teach humility, poverty, gentleness. And even more, as Thérèse rediscovered: to teach us to *love* humility and poverty as the conditions of the happiness of God. We are disarmed, so we are certain of victory.

We Are Thirsty for Happiness, but We Are Afraid of Being Thirsty

The Christian is called to be united with and to share in the beatitude of God; he soon sees the cross rise on his route; then he discovers that the latter is not only an obstacle: it is also a revelation of the beatitude to which he is invited; he begins then to dread this beatitude; but at the same time, he continues to desire it. And he can escape neither this fear nor this desire because he is wrestling with an excessive love that wishes to take possession of him.

Grace gives a thirst for God, for the beatitude of God and no other; the latter alone can henceforth satisfy our expectations, even if we do not know it. We can remain for a long time without knowing it, carry this seed for a long time in ourselves without its being very apparent from outside, as one carries a seed of life or death for years while continuing to lead an ordinary life and without suspecting anything. At the very most, an obscure uneasiness alerts us that in spite of a happy or passionate life, as they say, we are not satisfied; we take to dreaming now and then of something new, unforeseen, extraordinary, which never comes. One day this uneasiness becomes a call: we have perceived that something is waiting for us over there, very far away, and that this something is someone, and that this someone is God, the beatitude of God, a mystery that the eyes of man have not seen nor have his ears heard, something unheard of, unfathomable. Then "we leave Egypt", and we set off after Christ like a sheep following its shepherd, without knowing deep down where he is leading us, since we know nothing of this mysterious happiness that awaits us. We only know that it is happiness, that it is true, that it is ours, that for which we were made, and this is enough. That is the whole meaning of monastic enclosure. In thinking of Carmel, we cannot speak of a "prison" life, since those who are cloistered have chosen to separate themselves in order to love more profoundly.

Between Us and Happiness

At the beginning, anyway, the route is easy, and we are captivated by the journey itself. Undoubtedly we have read the Gospels, and we know there will be trials. But, in a word, we are in springtime. Then, one day, the words of the Gospels and of Saint Paul resonate with a new tone: "If anyone wishes to be my disciple, let him renounce himself, take up his cross, and follow me." When these words have passed into our flesh and blood like this, they are hard to bear! We are tempted to revolt against them on days when faith is more difficult. Hearing them is hard to tolerate then. And yet, it is the truth: Between us and our happiness, the only one we truly wanted, the cross arises, our cross, the only one we did not want.

Then we begin to be afraid, and we want to cheat. We reassure ourselves as well as we can. Sometimes we are weak, and we try to forget the hardness of the message inscribed in our hearts. Fine principles, moreover, are not lacking. Sometimes we feel strong and generous, and the temptation, which is more subtle and also more difficult to unmask, is to avoid the true situation. Our courage revives; we are excited at the generosity: "After all, it is a bad time to go on; let's be magnanimous, let's endure for the love of God what so many others have endured for less elevated motives; we can do nothing by ourselves, of course, but grace will never be lacking us if we are faithful and resolute. Help yourself, and heaven will help you; let us run so as to win the prize", and so on.

It Is Not Reserved for the Strong

All that is true, but the mystery of the Cross is more profound; we do not get away from it with generosity, even with the help of grace. That is the final stage that Thérèse helps us go through. It is not so easy as that—and, in a sense, it is not so difficult, either, for it is not reserved for the strong, and the weakest have access to it. It is much easier and much more difficult because, at bottom, the mystery of the Cross is not a mystery of power but a mystery of impotence. It is a victory, without doubt, but a victory that is not of this world, an invisible victory, a victory hidden from the eyes of the very one who wins it, a victory that has all the appearances and all the taste of a defeat, that is experienced as a defeat. The Cross is not a mystery of heroism, but a mystery of love. It does not consist in suffering with courage or even in suffering per se, but in being afraid of suffering; it does not consist in jumping over an obstacle, but in being crushed by it; not in being great or generous, but in being little and ridiculous in our own eyes; not in deploying virtue, but in seeing all our virtue put to flight and reduced to dust—and in accepting all this through love. And for accepting powerlessness through love; power is of no use—love is necessary. Then, it is not by gritting our teeth that we achieve this, because if we are capable of gritting our teeth, it is because we are strong, and insofar as we are strong—with that power—we do not yet know what the love of Jesus is. Christ did not grit his teeth in order to go to his Passion; he did not give himself from the heart; he truly knew that that was impossible. He simply said: "Father, let your will be done and not mine", which is of another order, of another world, of the world of love. That love is not in us. God must fill us with it; he himself must come to love in us.

*

This divine love is already eternal life, the sole aspect of eternal life that we can know here below—faith and hope will pass away, but charity will not pass away; it is therefore also something of the eternal beatitude; it is the beatitude of the earth, the happiness of loving truly, of loving to excess, of loving as God loves. And this happiness is so far from

satisfying us that it is at the origin of an intense thirst to see
God. We know that in heaven there will be no more shadows or tears, and we would really like to be there. We
cannot cease being thirsty on earth, thirsty for love or
thirsty for God. But there is, in love and in the very thirst it
engenders, a certain presence of the One whom we love,
which, even if we do not sense him and believe we have
been abandoned, is already a beatitude. In heaven, we will
not have any more desire to love: we will know only the
desire for God, a desire always fulfilled and always reborn.
On earth, until we have reached the degree of love for
which we are predestined, we groan not only toward the
possession of God, but also toward the possession of that
love which is our sole happiness here below. When Thérèse
understood that, it was no longer the Cross that could
frighten her, it was the infinity of God; and not only his
majesty, but his love, his happiness, that happiness that he
wants to make us share.

Who is this God, what is this love, what is this beatitude
that comes to be fixed on the Cross? Why this collapse, this
ignominy, this impotence? The question is too much for us; it
is not made for a human heart; it is more than we can ask or
even endure. No, my God, do not give us so much!

In Pursuit of a Moment's Happiness

And yet . . . It is not because we are afraid that we can stop
being thirsty or hearing the call of Christ: on the contrary, it
becomes more pressing than ever. Only he did not want to
fool us: he could not reveal the essence of his joy before
sharing it, but he wanted to say something about it. He
wanted us to know forever that it was not of this world.

The divine beatitude has lived among us; it has chosen a

dwelling place on earth, and that dwelling place is Jesus. There is no other. People are always looking for another, and they do not find it. We wander all over the earth in pursuit of happiness, in pursuit of a moment's happiness, but for every man there is one place, and only one, where he can find that happiness that he seeks everywhere by anxiously questioning landscapes, faces, and hearts; there is one moment, and only one, when he will be able to experience the consummation of all his thirst, which is a thirst to love, that is to say, a thirst for having thirst; that is the hour of Christ, his hour, the one that gives meaning to all the others and that all the others have, as a unique function, to prepare for, to fashion and slowly engender, just as all our *Paters*, all our *Aves*, all our liturgies, our *De Profundis* sink into and inscribe in us, day after day, the one *Pater*, the one *Ave*, the one cry of distress and of love that will spring forth one day finally from the depths of our heart and of our misery and that will irresistibly force the gate of heaven. The hour of our perfect joy will therefore also be that of our greatest anguish, for it is impossible on earth to possess both the appearance of happiness and its reality. Now, we have a thirst for its reality. Then we wait and we seek, and when it appears, we do not recognize it; or if we recognize it, then we no longer want it: it is too much for us. When we have rejected it, we understand that we have rejected happiness and that this will always be so, since we will always be thirsty, since we will not escape this thirst, since it pursues us, torments us, obsesses us, exhausts us. The love of God pursues us, in search of a heart that will open itself to him. Thérèse would not escape the weight that drew her toward him, because the thirst had been in her, as in us, since baptism: we have been marked there with the seal of love, and from that day, the last word has been said for us.

Perfect Joy

Only the exits of despair, anesthesia, or revolt remain—and
this is indeed what is most agonizing. For, in the end, when
we reach the banks of the Promised Land and we must
achieve our passage into God, when we discover in all its
truth and in all its nudity our condition as creature, we will
understand that divine beatitude bursts open the limits of our
heart and of our poor way of being happy and of conceiving
of happiness. Then how will we keep from drawing back?

That is why there is no other recourse but to root ourselves
in the spirit of childhood. We can be indifferent to the little
way of childhood; that is easy; there are grounds for it: we
need only stop at appearances and accidentals, at the "good
Sister" style and the cartoon characters, without penetrating
deeper. Let us not forget that the Incarnation consisted in
being placed within reach of men, of bending, when necessary, to their slowness and their weakness, so that they might
understand and love the essential point, the one thing necessary, God. The essence of the way of childhood is humble
and trusting docility to the spirit of God. He alone can
make us understand and taste that the Lord is gentle, that the
consuming fire he wishes to pass on is his very tenderness,
his maternal tenderness, peace beyond all sentiment, gentleness so intense and so profound that it transcends all violence, not through some other violence, but through its very
gentleness.

*

In the interminable wait for a sun that no longer rises,
Thérèse defined "perfect joy". In September 1896, in the

very midst of the crisis from which she would be freed only by death, she wrote:

> But is PURE LOVE in my heart? Are my measureless desires only but a dream, a folly? Ah! if this be so, Jesus, then enlighten me. . . . If my desires are rash, then make them disappear, for these desires are the greatest martyrdom to me. . . . Explain this mystery to me! . . . Oh no! the little bird will not even be troubled. . . . It wishes to remain gazing upon its Divine Sun. Nothing will frighten it, neither wind nor rain, and if dark clouds come and hide the Star of Love, the little bird will not change its place because it knows that beyond the clouds its bright Sun still shines on and that its brightness is not eclipsed for a single instant.
>
> At times the little bird's heart is assailed by the storm, and it seems it should believe in the existence of no other thing except the clouds surrounding it; this is the moment of *perfect joy* for the *poor little weak creature.* And what joy it experiences when remaining there just the same! and gazing at the Invisible Light which remains hidden from its faith! (SS 197–98)

APPENDIX 1

The Hope That Thérèse Might
Be Declared "Doctor of the Church"

Allow me to offer a few explanations and to render homage
to those to whom I owe a debt of gratitude I will never be
able to repay.

First of all, to the one who in 1944 was my father master of
novices, Father Chevignard. He had the wisdom to introduce
young Dominicans to the life of prayer by placing in their
hands the writings of Teresa of Avila and John of the Cross,
but in the light of Thérèse of Lisieux. The *Story of a Soul*, the
Novissima Verba, and the collection of Thérèse's thoughts and
words gathered by Mother Agnès under the title *The Spirit of
Thérèse of Lisieux* became our permanent prayer companions.
Ever since that year, I have never stopped discussing Saint
Thérèse of Lisieux with one of my companions in the novitiate, Father Molinié. This dialogue was a gift from heaven.

In 1949, by chance, when I was spending a year as deacon
in a German religious house and in that way reestablishing
some essential contacts interrupted by the war, I was able to
read with pen in hand the five hundred very dense pages of a
work that was to make a strong impression on me: *Des*

As previously noted, this work, published in 1996, anticipated by one year
the declaration of Saint Thérèse as Doctor of the Church made by Pope John
Paul II on October 19, 1997, World Day of Missions.—TRANS.

237

verborgene Antlitz [The hidden face], by Ida Friederike Görres, which was published by Herder in that same year, 1949. That this remarkable study written by a woman about Thérèse has not been translated [into French] still remains an enigma to me.[1] She had, like Father Petitot as early as 1925 and later Msgr. Combes, grasped the essence of Thérèse so well!

In 1953, when I was professor of dogmatic theology at the Saulchoir faculty, I had the joy of preaching, among others, retreats at the Carmels of Boulogne-sur-Seine and Tours. There, the mother prioress asked me to write a preface for the book by Louis Van den Bossche on *Le Message de Soeur Marie de Saint-Pierre*. In doing so, I discovered even more about the place that Sister Marie de Saint-Pierre and M. Dupont, the "holy man of Tours", held in Thérèse of Lisieux's devotion to the Holy Face. They had a very marked presence in the tradition of the Guérin and Martin families. Thérèse was inscribed in the confraternity of Tours, and she owed much of her devotion to the Holy Face to the influence of the Carmel of Tours. I had the text of this preface sent for her review to Sister Geneviève (Céline), the sister of Thérèse who was still living, and received a long and very lively letter from her.

Like all faithful readers of Thérèse of Lisieux, I received two shocks: that of the publication of the *Lettres* by Msgr. Combes in 1948 and that of the facsimile reproduction of the *Manuscrits autobiographiques* in 1956, under the supervision of Father François de Sainte-Marie, followed by the two volumes of photographs of the *Visage de Thérèse de Lisieux* at the beginning of the year 1961, the year that was to see the premature death of Father François in August.

---

[1] This work has been translated into English: *The Hidden Face: A Study of St. Thérèse of Lisieux*, trans. Richard and Clara Winston (New York: Pantheon, 1959)—TRANS.

In 1962, given responsibility by my superiors for the literary direction of Éditions du Cerf, one of my first initiatives was to take up my pilgrim's staff and head for Lisieux, where I asked the mother prioress of the Carmel if we might not republish *L'Esprit* and the letters of Thérèse, which were out of print. Later, a very dear friend, Father Albert Patfoort, a Dominican, entrusted to me the draft of the work begun by Father François de Sainte-Marie, which was unfortunately stopped by death and which was once again broken off when Father Delalande, the successor to Father François, had to assume the responsibility of provincial superior of the Carmelites. Providence allowed a novice who had just re-entered the Carmelites, in 1967, although he was already a priest, Father Guy Gaucher, the companion of a certain Father Lustiger, chaplain at the Sorbonne, to be available. At the same time, Msgr. Badré, who was to become bishop of Lisieux, asked me to be a part of his theological council as assistant bishop to the armed forces. The confidence of the mother prioress of the Carmel, of Bishop Badré, and of Father Guy Gaucher were to permit Sister Cécile, of the Lisieux Carmel, to place all her enthusiasm, her intelligence, and her unmatched precision at the service of the project of the centenary edition, which I was able, as director of Éditions du Cerf, to set in motion. Certainly, the latter accepted the desire of their director as a sweet but crazy whim. Of course, Lisieux existed. But for many "intellectuals", Thérèse in those years still seemed very secondary. It was only "spirituality" (cf. the very typical opinion of Father Karl Rahner). Sister Geneviève, a Dominican of Mortefontaine, became, along with Father Patfoort, a supporter, a helper, and an infinitely precious adviser, and also the faithful and personal friendship of Cardinal Paul Philippe and Cardinal Jérôme Hamer, both Dominicans, played a decisive role in the subsequent editions of Thérèse. The committee of sponsors was composed of Cardinal Garrone, Pierre Emmanuel, Professor Marrou, Dean Latreille, Jean Guitton, Father Urs von Balthasar, and others, who received in 1971 the first volume of the critical edition of the works of Thérèse, which owed everything to Sister Cécile and Guy Gaucher.

1973: The centenary of Thérèse's birth was a great date for all of us. Each cooperated in his own way. For my part, I had the joy of making Thérèse known through conferences in more than seventy cities: Cherbourg, Luxembourg, Dunkerque, Lyons, Rennes, Tours, Notre-Dame de Paris, and so on.

A thousand memories could be called forth by each occasion on Thérèse, for example, the joy of preaching a triduum and celebrations at the basilica and at the Carmel of Lisieux— among others those of the first centenary of her birth. I wish to record here two moments. After May 1968, France-Culture wished to take a break, and I was invited as a partner for several broadcasts for three voices, with André Frossard and Maurice Clavel. After one of the recordings, which had taken place in the common room of my religious house of that time, once the technicians had left, Clavel took me by the arm and led me into the little chapel, confiding to me: "Now come pray with me. The son of one of my friends has just committed suicide. I've been thinking about Thérèse of Lisieux all day. She's the only one who might understand." We then knelt in silence, praying to Thérèse.

The same thing was to happen again in different circumstances. I had just shared in a meal arranged by the person in charge of the bishops' secretariat for public opinion, along with Father Armogathe, who was a little reserved about the film *Thérèse*, directed by Alain Cavalier, although that film has delighted all "Thérèsians". The film maker, who was very discreet, had listened to Father Armogathe's objections. One single time, in order to respond secretly to all the questions others had asked him in order to find out if he was Catholic, Alain Cavalier knelt with me there where Clavel had, in silence. And he simply sent me the script of his film with his annotations. I keep it as a smile from Thérèse.

As early as 1969, a team had been established whose friendship, work, and fidelity was to be unfailing. It was composed, at the outset, of Guy Gaucher, who had since become bishop of Lisieux, Father Conrad De Meester, from whom I had welcomed the volume *Dynamique de la confiance* for the theological collection, Father Descouvemont, Father Michel Veys, and Father Gilbert Larsonneur, to whom were added with complete friendship and confidence, the three directors of the Lisieux pilgrimage, Msgr. Durand, Msgr. Gires, and Father Zambelli, and later the Carmelite Father Emmanuel Renault as well as Father Patrick-Dominique Linck, a Dominican. This little group functioned marvelously in total freedom, trust, and generosity. We alternated meetings for work on the texts and Thérèsian themes and brought in numerous reflections from an invited "expert". In this way a psychoanalyst, a Jesuit Hegelian, a Carmelite theologian, Jean Guitton, among others, came to give us their conclusions. Twice a year, these meetings allowed a free, fruitful, prayerful—in a word, Thérèsian—exchange. The goal was not to produce any particular thing, but to grow in understanding of the mystery.

But the editorial projects became more burdensome. In 1981, Sister Geneviève had rejoined Thérèse of Lisieux. Fortunately, providence allowed M. and Mme. Lonchampt to devote a large part of their time, their editorial skill, their care, and their affection over more than two decades to drawing up the plans for the centenary edition. These resulted in the one-volume publication of all the Thérèsian texts and in the boxed eight volumes of the critical edition, to which must be added the group of "Thérèsian studies", such as *La Passion de Thérèse de Lisieux*, by Guy Gaucher,[2] and *L'Épreuve de la foi* [Trial of faith], by Emmanuel Renault, and the two books of Thérèsian iconography by Father Descouvemont.

In 1973, I was asked to gather together intuitions, theological reflections, work plans, and wishes for Thérèse of Lisieux in a little volume for the "Epiphany" collection. I entitled it *La Gloire et le mendiant* [Glory and the beggar]. It was quickly out of print, but I did not want to go back to it before the definitive editions were established. The approach of the second centenary led me to regroup the work, taken up again completely anew after twenty-three years. I am especially indebted, for this work, to three people. It would be necessary to name them on every page. Allow me to repeat my immense gratitude to them: to Bishop Guy Gaucher for the first part on the family; to Father Descouvemont, for the second part on God; to Father De Meester, for the third part on the message. Saint Thérèse has already taken them, in her own way, into her "shower of roses". I know that she will continue. All of us are hopeful that Thérèse will be declared a "doctor of the Church".

Many theologians since 1932, following Father Desbuquois, have expressed reasons for which it would be good to have Thérèse declared "Doctor". This grace would not call her

[2] This work has been published in English as *The Passion of Thérèse of Lisieux*, with a new intro. by Benedict J. Groeschel (New York: Crossroad, 1998).—TRANS..

doctrine into question. There is no need to. The proof of the
eminent quality of that doctrine has been given for seventy
years. But this declaration would powerfully help toward a
new equilibrium in theology, first of all in its scientific role
as light for the Church and as a telephone operator, if I
might put it that way, for the transmission of the faith. The
life and works of Thérèse of Lisieux move us off center and
oblige us to find our bearings once again, at least on several
decisive points broached in this book, which we will recall in
concluding:

—The trinitarian life, the source and end of all human life
even here on earth.

—The radical newness of Jesus' coming and the Incarnation and, therefore, the importance of the everyday in the
very name of the transcendence of God, and not only in
facing God (when it is not "against" him, as if he were a
competitor). From this followed, for Thérèse, her lucid love
of the Church in her institution itself.

—A morality based on the imitation of Christ, not only
because he is the "horizon of man", but because he is the
Word of God, revealing and inviting every human being to
imitate the "ways" of his Father and to receive the fruits of
the Spirit. Through her understanding of love, Thérèse returns to the whole dynamism of the virtues its true divine,
and not only human, stature.

—The unity of a contemplative *and* missionary life by its
trinitarian and filial source. Thérèse leads beyond an anony-
mous Christianity that would remain at the level of proposing
the Beatitudes as if they were one more social or humanitar-
ian movement, without theological roots in contemplation of
the living God.

—The role of "works", the meaning of offering all sufferings and all sacrifices, thus giving a meaning to merit,

because, thanks to the "little way", such merits have reality only within a life of abandonment and trust. In coming back to the audacity of God, "a beggar in Jesus Christ", Thérèse abolished all stoicism, all puritanism, all Jansenism, and all Pelagianism. She transfigured all fear into an opportunity to hand oneself over. Gone was the myth of the Christian "adult". Long live the children of God!

—The reality of hope at the heart of a world without reference points.

—Finally, the only possible and truly universal ecumenism, beyond even the religions of the Book and of the different figures of monotheism: the communion and ecumenism drawn from mercy, understood not only as a compassion that would be but an accident of God, but as the center of his inner life and the source of the originality of all Christian mysteries.

Thérèse provided an introductory work to the "practice" of theology in that she obliged three essential tasks of any catechism and of any exposition of the Christian mystery: (1) the purification of our ideas so that they do not diminish God; (2) the manifestation of the coherence of and the connections between the mysteries; and, (3) finally, the proof of their nourishing value and of the possibility of a universal and "catholic" language of faith. With the Curé of Ars, would Thérèse not be the best guide in reading the Second Vatican Council and what followed?

Thérèse of Lisieux, Joan of Arc, and the Mystics

The human mind quickly becomes irritated when faced with something it cannot dissolve into simple ideas, with what resists it or seems to escape its a priori schemas. It is normal for it to be concerned with remaining master of its thought. To do so, two solutions are common: either we diminish the things to the measure of our experience, or else we decide that they are not real and we drop them. This is standard practice, as prevalent in the history of art or in the history of the Church or of mysticism as when it is a matter of explaining some affective phenomenon. There is perhaps a third possibility. One that would respect the proper nature of the object in question even if it means admitting being surpassed by it. This is the case with all knowledge of faith. We cannot leave our relationship with God in order to speak of God, since that relationship constitutes our very being. Knowledge of the object of faith, whether it is a question of God, of Christ, of the Church, or of mysticism, in order to be truly discerned, presupposes that we adhere with "sympathy" to that object. Otherwise, whatever is specific to it eludes at the very root the descriptions and analyses we would like to give it. Those who refuse this sympathy are like the deaf man who, having arrived at the edge of his tomb, perceives that he has spoken of music without ever hearing it. We will always need to mobilize the understanding of the heart anew in order to speak of what in the end falls within the province of the attachment of the heart. Pascal has admirably and definitively said it. If Father Karl Rahner is "irritated", "nauseated", or "bored" by Thérèse of Lisieux, as we recalled in our introduction, is that the fault of Thérèse? Once again, in order to get hold of a reality that surpasses us, the temptation is normally to use interpretive frameworks that reduce that reality. It is easy to find argumentation and motives to flatten, dull, or justify our descriptions.

Thérèse of Lisieux is in the same situation as Joan of Arc. Both illustrate very well this phenomenon of interpretation and furnish a surprising test of it. It is enough to refer to the eight columns of the *Encyclopaedia Universalis* devoted to Joan of Arc or to the edition of the *Procès de condamnation* in the "Archives" series (Gallimard), in order to find simplisms, anachronisms, indeed, inaccurate translations from the pen of "reputed" historians. What is to be said of the way in which the voices and the vocation of Joan of Arc are explained in the scholarly textbooks? Régine Pernoud has drawn up a balance sheet of some meaningless generalities and outrageous mistakes on the subject of Joan of Arc in a book of exemplary accuracy and pungency: *Jeanne face aux Cauchons.*[1] When will we have the equivalent of such a study for Thérèse of Lisieux, in which its humor would rival its erudition? We must not be surprised if it is the same for these two as it was for Christ, for the Gospels, and for the Resurrection. There will always be Athenians to say to Saint Paul, after his discourse on the Acropolis, in which he had spoken

[1] Paris: Seuil, 1978.

of the risen Christ: "You interest us, but come back tomorrow." Here, respect for what is in question does not spring first and solely from learning but from a minimum of connaturality, from sympathy with and respect for what is at issue. To speak of the Cistercians of the Middle Ages, a few days sharing life with Trappists in their monastery can perhaps teach as much as an examination of cartularies. It would prevent such a medievalist from concluding that Cistercian abbeys of today are no longer anything but "empty shells" . . . while more than three hundred of them still remain, full of life, praise, silence, truth, and devotion. Must we wait until the television news announces the assassination of seven Trappist monks at Médéa in Algeria in order to realize this?

To approach Thérèse of Lisieux, a certain familiarity with monastic life helps as much as long semantic, psychological, or structuralist research. It was for me an opportunity and a gift from heaven for which I can never give sufficient thanks to have preached the full annual eight-day retreat and to have been confessor at more than 110 abbeys, convents, and monasteries, of both men and women, on five continents (in sum, the equivalent of more than two years of my life), many of which were Carmels: Avranches at Besançon, Beauvais at Saint-Germain-en-Laye, Pontoise and Boulogne-sur-Seine, and so on, and to have received the trust, confidences, and reflections of religious living the same life as Thérèse of Lisieux.

I have been able to glimpse a little of the music of Thérèse, of her joy, her faith, her night, and her hope, not only in reading or analyzing the musical score with the critical examination of her manuscripts, but in seeing the same fervor, the same combat, the same trust live in others. Saint Francis de Sales said that "there is between the Gospel text and the

life of the saints as much difference as between musical notation and sung music."

That confirms for me the decisive importance of the choice
between a "reductive" hermeneutics and a hermeneutics that
"builds up" when it comes to analyzing sanctity. It is easy to
understand this distinction between two fundamentally di-
vergent mental attitudes. We have recalled that the first, in
order to grasp what is real, reduces it and employs suspicion as
its method of investigation; the second considers it better to
understand a reality by seeking what is positive about it and
by going all the way with this positive aspect, even if it
surpasses our mind. This presupposes that, in the place of
doubt, we strive first of all for an authentic connaturality and
sympathy with the reality being studied. We have already
twice explained this at length, in 1967, with respect to the
sacraments,[2] and in 1995, in regard to the mystery of Christ.[3]
The admissions by the founder of structuralism about the
disinterest he feels for the religious heritage received from his
family and others among his rabbinic relatives are pathetic
when he affirms at the same time that the mystics represent
for him a category that excites his curiosity. Would they be
reduced to the state of "structures"?

It is useful to return to this fundamental distinction in order
to understand the approaches of those interested in Thérèse
of Lisieux. Very interesting suggestions will be found in Gilbert Durand, *L'Imagination symbolique*,[4] and, by the same author, *Les Structures anthropologiques de l'imaginaire*.[5]   The

[2] In *L'Homme et les sacrements* (Paris: Cerf, 1967), pp. 420ff.
[3] In *Peut-on éviter Jésus-Christ?* (Paris: Éd. de Fallois, 1995), pp. 263–97.
[4] Paris: PUF, 1964.
[5] Paris: PUF, 1964.

philosopher Ricoeur has often returned to it, for example, in his essay on Freud: *De L'interprétation*.[6] Rather than give details about Thérèse that it would be easy to find and that everyone already knows, let us cite the "reductive" hermeneutics that Gilbert Durand analyzes: for example, Freud, Barthes, Lévi-Strauss, Vernant, and so on, and the hermeneutics that "builds up": Cassirer, Bachelard, and so on. Suspicion can sometimes be interesting, but what does it become if it is not supported by an intelligent sympathy? Besides Christ, the sacraments, sanctity, and the mystics, we could take a thousand other examples: the analysis of a phenomenon such as the paintings of Lascaux and prehistoric religions; the self-portraits of Rembrandt as well as the evolution of the liturgy and of church architecture before and after the Council. Each time we find proof that complicity generates more knowledge than the dialectics of suspicion. Thérèse is a brilliant example of this.

The history of art furnishes a good laboratory and a useful analogy in order to situate the different approaches to mysticism and sanctity. Schematizations. We can recognize three types of aesthetics. There are, first of all, that which is based on memory of the imaginary. One takes stock, compares, contrasts: for example, Émile Mâle, Berenson, Volnay. Secondly, there is the aesthetics, particularly in university circles, that is primarily preoccupied with formal analyses, like that of Focillon, Federico Zeri, and Georges Duby. Finally, a third group takes the first two into account but goes much farther. This is the aesthetics that poses the question of destiny and of the meaning of works; this is what André Malraux, for example, does in *Les Voix du silence*, *La Métamorphose des dieux*,

---

[6] Paris: Seuil, 1965.

La Tête d'obsidienne, and the great trilogy *L'Intemporel, Le Surnaturel, L'Irréel,* as well as works by authors such as Kenneth Clarke, Jacques Maritain, René Huyghe, and Dominique Ponnau.

Would it be wrong to apply this interpretive framework to Thérèse of Lisieux? Bishop Guy Gaucher and Father Pierre Descouvemont have done a marvelous job of giving us an account of Thérèse. Father Conrad De Meester has done remarkably well in situating her destiny. As for those who strive for formal analyses . . . we willingly leave to each the task of gathering what might truly be useful.

APPENDIX 3

Thérèse: Jesus or Buddha?

Allow me one final detail, one that is essential when dealing with Thérèse of Lisieux. It might be entitled "Thérèse and Love", as an introduction to chapter 6.

In order to avoid the error of some biographers, even those with good intentions, like Jean Chalon, we can never repeat enough that if the secret of Thérèse is love, the secret of love is not the idolatry of love but the object of desire toward whom or toward which love attracts us. This is what makes radically illusory the biographies of Thérèse that proceed no farther than descriptions of love on the psychological or psychoanalytical order. One does not write a life of Thérèse of Lisieux as if one were describing the life of someone on the fringes of late nineteenth-century society. A distinction is indispensable here. The essential character of love, of hate, of fear, of hope, or of desire is the attention toward its object. To focus primarily on someone's mood, on his love or his fear, is to cease focusing on the object loved or feared. In other words, we cannot both enjoy and contemplate interior activities at the same time. We cannot, at the same time, hope and think about hope; for in hoping, we think of the object of hope, but we are interrupted (so to speak) when we turn our eye toward the hope itself. These two activities can of course alternate (and they do) very rapidly; but they are distinct and incompatible.

The surest means of deflating anger or desire is to divert our attention from the person loved or the insult received to examine the passion itself. The surest means of spoiling a pleasure is to set about observing our own satisfaction. In introspection we try to look "into ourselves" in order to see what is happening. This is, in some ways, always somewhat false. Everything that was happening an instant before is stopped by the very fact that we are observing it. Introspection finds what remains when our normal activities are suspended, which is to say, principally mental images and physical sensations. The great error is to take our impressions, our moods, which are only mere sediments, imprints, and by-products, to be the activity of love itself. The dual division into "conscious" and "unconscious" is insufficient. It should be threefold: conscious, unconscious, and "contemplated". Thérèse of Lisieux is an incomparable master in helping us see to what degree it is the object of love that has priority and not the idolatry of needing to love or to be loved. Thérèse did not merely love to love. She loved Someone who threw her whole life off-center, and she accepted being off-center, losing herself in him and for him, responding to his good pleasure. Now the one she loved was not just anyone; he is himself uniquely turned by love toward his Father. She did not pray to or love "a" God, but the Word and the Father who gave her his Son. Thus Thérèse surrendered to a movement that is centrifugal; her conversion consisted in reversing the movement that led her to look at herself. If, in a biography of Thérèse, one can interchange the name of Jesus, for example, with that of Buddha, without anything being changed, then we do not have there the love to which Thérèse gave herself. Thérèse did not pursue images and sensations of love for themselves. She knew that these were only traces left in her by the passage of Joy and of Divine

Love—not the wave, but only its imprint on the sand. Thérèse is here the master of life when she shows how desire is not turned toward self but toward its object; what is more, desire owes its whole character to that object. Thérèse does not seek the divine. She seeks God, and that is something entirely different. It is desire that gives a form to its object. It is the object that renders the desire hard or soft, coarse or refined, noble or trivial. It is the object that renders the desire itself desirable or detestable. A miracle is necessary on heaven's part; a conversion on ours. This is what Thérèse proposes.